Instructor's Manual

Steps to Writing Well

ELEVENTH EDITION

and

Steps to Writing Well
with Additional Readings

EIGHTH EDITION

Jean Wyrick

Professor Emerita, Colorado State University

Jean Wyrick

Additional Material by
Christi Conti

WADSWORTH
CENGAGE Learning™

Australia • Brazil • Japan • Korea • Mexico • Singapore • Spain • United Kingdom • United States

ISBN-13: 978-0-495-90367-3
ISBN-10: 0-495-90367-1

Wadsworth
20 Channel Center Street
Boston, MA 02210
USA

Cengage Learning is a leading provider of customized learning solutions with office locations around the globe, including Singapore, the United Kingdom, Australia, Mexico, Brazil, and Japan. Locate your local office at: **www.cengage.com/global**

Cengage Learning products are represented in Canada by Nelson Education, Ltd.

To learn more about Wadsworth, visit **www.cengage.com/wadsworth**

Purchase any of our products at your local college store or at our preferred online store **www.CengageBrain.com**

For product information and technology assistance, contact us at **Cengage Learning Customer & Sales Support, 1-800-354-9706**

For permission to use material from this text or product, submit all requests online at www.cengage.com/permissions Further permissions questions can be emailed to **permissionrequest@cengage.com**

READ IMPORTANT LICENSE INFORMATION

Printed in the United States of America
2 3 4 5 6 7 13 12 11 10

CONTENTS

Overview of *Steps to Writing Well*

Part One—The Basics of the Short Essay provides fundamental instruction for college-level writing expectations, addressing all aspects of the writing process from prewriting through final draft, with discussion and practice sessions that employ strategies for drafting and revision. In addition, introductions to creative and critical thinking, effective sentence construction, word logic, and connections between reading and writing link students to essential details in the writing process while giving them the language to talk about writing. Equipped with these tools, students can begin to effectively negotiate the more detailed instruction and advice that Part Two—Purposes, Modes, and Strategies illustrates, while putting to use new skills and knowledge gained from Part One.

Part Two emphasizes strategies for developing ideas and text, organizing text, analyzing text, and assessing and revising text. The major focus in this section involves developing text based upon audience needs and purposes for writing. While this section covers four basic strategies—exposition, argumentation, description, and narration—Wyrick clarifies that most writing does not exist in "any one mode in a pure form."

Rather, most writing reflects a writer's primary goal or purpose, i.e., an argument or a story, but entails a combination of writing types/strategies throughout. Once students begin to recognize the structural elements of each type, they can begin to employ the elements logically at all stages of the writing process—prewriting (discovery of topics, theses, audiences, purposes, and content), drafting, and revision. Chapter 13 ends this section with a discussion of combining elements, analysis of an essay using multiple strategies, and as in all other chapters, practice and suggestions for writing.

Part Three—Special Assignments focuses on writing scenarios that students will encounter in college and beyond, familiarizing them more fully with 1) college-level writing and research methods, strategies, and formats, including using library and online sources; 2) practical advice on how to respond effectively to timed writing prompts, with special emphasis on the "Response" essay; 3) basic ways to read, analyze, and write about short stories and poetry; 4) additional perspectives on ways to assess and write about film and film reviews; 5) the do's and don'ts of business writing, covering such elements as memos, letters, e-mail, and résumés; and 6) a chapter that explains ways to write about the visual arts of painting, sculpture, and photography. Students have an opportunity to apply this chapter's advice to the many visuals within *Steps*. Likewise, instructors hoping to cover each of the major concerns in this section can easily develop units using the topics here as themes—text-response, research, literature, work—incorporating chapters from other sections as appropriate. For instance, Chapters 8 (The Reading-Writing Connection), 9 (Exposition), 23 (Development by Example), and 25 (Comparison/Contrast) could comprise a unit on text-response or timed writing. Add Chapters 16 and 33 (both of which focus on poems and short stories) and a unit on literature is born. Chapters 10 (Argumentation), 13 (Writing Essays Using Multiple Strategies), 26, 27, 28, and 29 will build a strong scaffold for both analyzing and creating arguments. Finally, teachers wanting to incorporate work themes into their classrooms can begin or end a term with Chapter 19, asking students to create real résumés.

Part Four—A Concise Handbook offers support for those students needing to sharpen their grammar and punctuation skills.

Part Five—Additional Readings includes eleven chapters of added readings, illustrating exposition, argumentation, description, narration, multiple strategies, and literature. These chapters can be used in conjunction with Part Two reading assignments, either through themes suggested within the essays or through organizational considerations, as Wyrick's text seems to suggest. In addition, should instructors choose to create units based on suggestions here about Part Three—Special Assignments, the additional readings will provide a variety of examples for further in-depth analysis and discussion. Wyrick has chosen challenging texts that offer not only clear examples of writing strategies and processes, but interesting, timely, and perhaps timeless topics for discussion.

4

Suggested Teaching Tools to Use with *Steps to Writing Well*

The composition maxim "The only way to learn to write is by writing and rewriting" is underscored in *Steps* as emphasis is placed on writing and revision through creative and critical thinking (Chapter 5). Keeping journals (Chapter 1) and participating in collaborative activities (Chapter 5) are two ways instructors might encourage students to examine their own writing process and analyze the writing of others, enabling them to bring new insights to their own work.

■ The Journal

Chapter 1 of *Steps to Writing Well* discusses the benefits of keeping a journal and offers students suggested uses for the journal. Jean Wyrick notes that there are numerous advantages in requiring a journal:

Benefits for the student:

- encourages thinking, learning, discovery
- helps sequence the student's writing processes—provides practice of skills
- improves the quality of the written product—reduces writing anxiety
- improves class participation

Benefits for the teacher:

- provides opportunities to intervene in the students' composing stages
- ensures better "products" to evaluate
- may replace traditional assignments
- may reduce grading time and pressure
- discourages "passive" reading of assigned material
- allows the monitoring of class progress, understanding of material

For journals to be an effective part of a college composition course, expectations for journal assignments should be clearly communicated to the students. The journal provides them with a chance to write informally, perhaps experimenting with their writing and taking more risks than they would in a traditional, formal essay assignment. This is not to say, however, that journals are not to be taken seriously by student writers: if journals are to be a success, with assignments that are rewarding for the instructor as well as the students, there should be accountability. When students are thoroughly invested in their journals, a great deal of learning can take place, but if the journal is not incorporated into class discussion and reviewed periodically by the instructor, the journal's effectiveness is likely to be diminished. Here is a sample description of a journal from one composition teacher's course guide:

> In much the same way that an artist uses a sketchbook to record ideas and preliminary sketches for larger works, your journal is a tool for you to document your ideas and progress in the writing field over the course of the semester. Assignments for the journal will be varied and will take place both in and out of class. A couple of notes: be sure to title and date each assignment, doing them in the order they are assigned. In addition to written assignments, class notes should also be recorded in the journal. In short, your journal should be a complete record of your preliminary writings for each

essay. A suggestion: consider reserving the last few pages of your journal to record assignments for each class meeting.

Structure

Please organize your journal by unit, labeling the first section "Introduction." As we complete each unit and move on to the next, title each section according to the writing strategy currently being explored ("Narration," "Description," etc.).

Grading

Journals will be collected at the conclusion of each unit, often the last class before an essay is due, and will be returned the following class period. Each assignment will be noted as complete or incomplete, with credit given for each thoroughly completed assignment. At the end of the term, your journal grade will be determined as a percentage (number completed out of the number possible) and converted to a letter grade.

When giving take-home journal assignments, detailed instructions help guarantee completed, thorough journal entries. Here is a sample assignment:

Journal Assignment Three

For most of this course, we have been discussing the importance of writing clear, straightforward essays that communicate directly to the reader. These were characterized by unity, coherence, a clear, narrow focus, effective paragraph development, and creative introductions and conclusions.

For this journal assignment, choose a *cover story* from any *Time* or *Newsweek* magazine. Then do the following:

- Copy it on a copy machine and staple it to this assignment sheet. Make sure the entire article is included.

- Use a pen or pencil to mark up the essay (unmarked essays are not acceptable). Make note of things like transitional devices, thesis statements, interesting concrete language, paragraph development, etc. In other words, try to notice as many of the concepts we talked about in class as possible.

- In the margin or somewhere near each mark, identify what it is you are marking.

- On a separate sheet of paper, write four or five sentences evaluating the essay, making some comment about the audience for which the essay is intended, the transitional devices used, and in general how you would evaluate the overall quality of the writing, based, again, on the things we have been discussing in class.

■ Computer Activities

For those who have access to computers in a classroom setting, any number of the Practice sessions, Writing Assignments, or activities listed in the text can be effectively translated into lessons that employ computer use.

1. Classroom discussion can take place through a variety of online forums or bulletin boards, or even e-mail if circumstances permit.

2. Prewriting, which asks students to explore ideas and to find connections, often suffers from the urge to edit. Ask students to practice free writing in class and/or at home or a computer lab while turning off the computer screen. Some will be discomfited by this activity as it prevents the flow of thought

from being maintained in the normal fashion—writing, pausing to read what one has written, editing, etc.

Instead, the writer is forced to simply put down whatever comes to mind, even if that means not finishing thoughts. Freewriting in this fashion can generate a good deal of brainstorming that may or may not appear as completed text, but that is the intent—to generate material that one can later formulate into comprehensible text for a reader. This activity is a wonderful tool for the writer who has trouble "getting started," but it needs to be practiced regularly for the writer to be able to overcome his or her discomfort.

3. Most word processing software includes some type of template for outlines. These templates can be utilized easily in both brainstorming and organization workshops suggested in Chapter 1— Prewriting. Meanwhile, presentation programs, such as PowerPoint, provide written guidelines for text development. Moreover, PowerPoint itself allows for creative presentation of student text, and is especially useful to introduce students to electronic and multimedia forums for oral reports. Web pages, home pages, and the like require a bit more computer knowledge than some students have, so presentation software is an easier way to incorporate the principles of reader/audience-centered text development. Moreover, incorporating presentations into class content enables students to recognize more readily the benefits of audience analysis as well as the connection between text and context.

4. If Internet access is available, the most obvious benefit for first-year students will be easy access to research materials. Moreover, research itself can be not just a unit of study, but an essential or core element in the class, included in each assignment in some fashion. Ready access to libraries provides students with immediate access to biographical and historical data that may assist them to understand obscure references in readings, to gather additional information about authors, places, times, etc. Meanwhile, learning to incorporate sources while working in Chapter 14 can be enhanced by continued practice in doing so and by instant access to online handbooks and style formats when other such texts are not available.

■ Collaborative Activities

In Chapter 5 of *Steps to Writing Well,* students are given advice on maximizing the effectiveness of revision workshops. There are also guidelines for the composition instructor to ensure successful collaborative activities. Jean Wyrick offers the following advice:

Suggestions for Organizing Collaborative Activities

Small-group work and peer revision workshops sometimes aren't as productive as we'd like them to be. Here are some suggestions for organizing collaborative activities that you might find useful.

1. Hand out a sample student paper the class session before the workshop. Ask students, at home, to write a brief summary and to make a note of the paper's major strengths and weaknesses. Ask them to bring this paper, their notes, and their own drafts to class.

2. Hand out written instructions for the workshop or write them on the board before class. At the top of the sheet/board include a statement of your (realistic, limited) goals for this activity.

3. Discuss your goals with the class. Talk about the value of giving and taking constructive criticism. (What kinds of comments are most helpful, which aren't, etc.?) Go over the instructions for the workshop *before* they move into pairs or groups.

4. Clearly state in writing an "accountability factor." Students must always know they are responsible for producing something that will be shared with the entire class at the end of the activity—a report, something to be written on the board, a reading of a revision, something.

5. State the time limit for this activity. (Tell them less time than you really can allow for this activity.) Fifteen to twenty minutes on one activity is probably tops. Always leave yourself maximum time to discuss the results of the activity. Whole-class discussion time should always be as long as (or longer than) the group time.

6. Always design the groups and match up students for pair work. Avoid matching buddies. Keep track of who is working with whom from week to week.

7. If you're doing small-group work, assign jobs: a recorder to keep notes, a timekeeper to move folks along, a reporter to present results, a facilitator to lead discussion, a "devil's advocate" to introduce a different point of view, and so on. Make each member of the group responsible for something.

8. Discuss the instructions for the workshop. If you're running a revision workshop, the instructions should be a limited number of clearly defined, specific tasks. Too many tasks addressing every aspect of the paper do not produce good results!

9. A note on the nature of the tasks: avoid simple yes/no questions (Is this paragraph adequately developed? "Yup"). It is frequently easier for students who are insecure about their ability to critique to offer advice after they have described what they see. Example: Underline the main thought of this paragraph. Number the specific examples (pieces of evidence, whatever) that support this idea. Would the paragraph profit from additional support? Why or why not? If yes, where?

10. Model the tasks on the sample student essay that you handed out last class. Modeling the responses shows students what you expect and also builds confidence in their ability to address these tasks and to critique a peer's paper.

11. Allow students to add at least one question to the list of tasks. They may do this as a class, or if they're in pairs, each student may add one individually. (As the semester progresses, the class should gradually take over the list of tasks.)

12. Circulate as they work. Move quietly from group to group. Listen, ask questions, but try not to assume leadership of the group. Note any common problems you might want to address at the end of the activity. Announce the time; give nearing-the-end warnings when appropriate ("Ten minutes left—you should have finished the first three tasks by this time").

13. Put the class back together as a whole and call for the results from some of the groups/pairs. Discuss the results and then demand that students apply wisdom gleaned from the activity to their own papers. Actual hands-on revision is best, but oral responses are good if you're short on time.

14. Always allow students to have the last word on the activity. Why was/wasn't it helpful? How could it be improved next time? These make good journal questions, especially if students want to complain about a partner who wasn't giving useful feedback.

15. When the papers are revised, let the peer-editor have a read before the papers come in. A quick read-and-pass is also fun—interesting too, how the papers get better when students know many of their peers will be reading them.

16. Have many, many workshops on a paper, not just one huge one toward the end. Vary the kinds of questions/tasks: reader-based, criterion-based, descriptive, evaluative, and so on. Fit the workshops to the stage of the writing process—one on purpose and audience, one on organization and development, one on mechanics—whatever fits your purpose, your students, and the assignment.

17. After you've read through the papers, consider "publishing" some of the better efforts or read them aloud. You don't always have to reprint an entire essay—you can also present the class with a list of effective sentences, phrases, images, or even "A+" action verbs that were direct hits!

Here is a sample assignment sheet for a small-group activity focusing on the argumentative essay "Students, Take Note!" (Chapter 10):

"Students, Take Note!": A Group Perspective

Instructions: As a group, discuss and answer each of the following questions. Choose a recorder to jot down group decisions, a facilitator to lead your group's discussion, a timekeeper (you'll have 15 minutes for this activity), and a reporter to present your findings to the class.

1. Consider the author's thesis. What evidence does the author give to support his or her claim? Why is/isn't this evidence effective? Where is the author most convincing? Least convincing?

2. Does the author acknowledge/refute opposition to his or her claim? Why is/isn't this effective? What are some arguments against the author's claim that the essay does not acknowledge?

3. Are there any logical fallacies in the essay? If so, identify them.

4. What is your group's assessment of the overall effectiveness of the essay?

■ Suggestions for Effective Essay Assignments

Student writers may have faced an assignment with a vague verbal statement of topic, length, and due date. The students in this case are left with a bewildering array of questions. How should the paper be developed? Is research required? How formal should the presentation be? These unanswered questions often lead to confusion and writer's block, resulting in a last-minute "shot in the dark" paper that does not accurately reflect the student's writing ability. In short, vague assignments often yield unsuccessful essays; thorough assignments encourage clear and effective student responses. To revise a well-known phrase, "As composition teachers sow, so shall they reap."

While classroom discussions, activities, and *Steps to Writing Well* will provide students with thorough guidelines for approaching a variety of writing strategies and styles, an effective essay assignment is vital to ensuring that student writers are able to transfer what they have learned in class and from the text to their own writing. Instructor's expectations for major essay assignments should be clearly established, preferably in a printed form that students can refer to throughout their writing process.

Here is a sample assignment sheet for an argumentative essay requiring research:

Argumentative Essay Assignment

Argumentative skills are a part of everyday life: on a daily basis, each of us makes claims about issues large or small. Consider the argumentative elements of issues that you're concerned about. To make this assignment a meaningful and successful endeavor, choose a topic of narrow scope so you can successfully support your stance. Consider the following guideline for your selection: avoid global issues and claims that are supported more by emotion or faith than fact. The key to a successful argumentative essay is to combine facts with logic to form a convincing argument.

Once you've selected a topic, examine the subject for a debatable claim. If the claim is arguable (is there an opposing side?) you have the focus for an argumentative essay. To clarify your purpose and goals for writing this essay, it is vital to define a specific audience.

Argumentative essays must be fully supported with a combination of personal perspective and research. This is a research paper: in addition to personal knowledge you must use the following support for your claim:

1. a minimum of 5 written sources to provide current, relevant support for your paper. Attach a photocopy or print-out of all sources to rough draft.

2. an interview with an authority on the subject

Essay Length: 4–7 pages, plus Works Cited page

<u>Due Dates</u>
Topic proposal presentation/review: Tues. 4/14 and Thurs. 4/16
Completed rough draft due for take-home peer review: Tues. 4/28
In-class workshop on rough draft: Thurs. 4/30
Final draft: Tues. 5/5

For particularly demanding assignments, a follow-up "suggestion" sheet, guiding writers away from pitfalls the instructor has often seen in student essays, is sometimes helpful as students work to select a topic.

Guidelines for Selecting a Successful Argumentative Essay Topic

1. Is the topic narrow enough to be successfully and convincingly developed in a 4–7- page essay? A very specific topic, well presented, is more effective than a broad (if seemingly more significant) topic that can't be developed fully.

2. Is there a legitimate opposition?

3. Can you refute the opposition's argument?

4. Can your position be argued and supported primarily with fact and logic rather than emotion, faith, or a morality-based stance?

5. Is it an issue you have experience with or have a vested interest in? To be convincing, your voice must be heard.

Topics to Avoid

1. Issues that have been argued for years (e.g., capital punishment or the drinking age) unless you have a new angle on an old topic.

2. Issues that you feel so passionately about that you can't argue your position logically (rather than emotionally) or acknowledge arguments of the opposition.

After students have selected a topic and have begun drafting, a detailed reminder of essay criteria can be a valuable resource. A criteria sheet like the following sample not only provides student writers with a self-assessment tool, it can also be used in peer workshops as a tool for reviewing the writing of others. Finally, the instructor can use this same sheet as a grading guideline.

Argumentative Essay Criteria Sheet

I. **FOCUS/THESIS**

    Clearly stated? _____

    Appropriate for scope of essay? _____

    Established as arguable topic? _____

II. **AUDIENCE**

    Strong sense of audience/purpose? _____

III. **SUPPORT FOR CLAIM**

    Each statement of opinion/assertion supported convincingly? _____

    A logical rather than emotional base for argument? _____

    Avoidance of logical fallacies? _____

    Convincing support of overall claim? _____

    Acknowledgment/refutation of opposition's claim? _____

IV. **STRUCTURE**

    Logical, coherent structure? _____

V. **USE OF SOURCES**

    Use of required research sources? _____

    Effective use of sources as support? _____

    Context/introduction of authority? _____

VI. **MLA/APA CITATION FORMAT**

    Correct format for in-text citations? _____

    Sources acknowledged appropriately? _____

    Correct Works Cited or References format? _____

VII. **MECHANICS**

    Free of mechanical errors? _____

VIII. **OTHER CONSIDERATIONS**

    Appropriate title? _____

    Effective lead-in? _____

    Clear transitions? _____

    Meaningful conclusion? _____

    Overall maintenance of focus/coherence/unity and development? _____

■ A Few Notes on Portfolio Grading

Many times an instructor looks at a student paper and thinks something like, "If Mary just had one more shot at this assignment, she'd have it," or "With some additional evidence, this would be a darned good argument!" How many times, after a week or more of rest from a project, has Mary been able to look at what she's written and then make similar comments about her own work?

Because of the typical structure of a composition class, however, teacher and student too often have to settle for what can be accomplished in a given time frame. To combat these somewhat arbitrary and frustrating limitations, instructors now sometimes turn to portfolio grading, or more appropriately, portfolio writing. In a portfolio class, students write and revise assignments continuously throughout the term and submit a final collection of their essays for a course grade. The obvious idea is that students can achieve better results with the benefit of time and perspective to help them revise. In this way, then, portfolio grading is one way to match class structure more closely to current *process* writing theory. Students can be evaluated on their cumulative efforts, on their overall assimilation of class concepts, and on their revising ability.

Portfolio writing can be integrated into class structure in a variety of ways. A student's grade might depend, for instance, on one final review of his or her portfolio with no grades given on any writing to that point. Comments on drafts might include general strengths and weaknesses or notes regarding specific mechanical issues you are working on in class, but no score is suggested. Students are encouraged by this system to focus more on their process than just on the outcome. Instead of meeting an artificial deadline established only by the syllabus and a teacher's need to space assignments efficiently throughout the term, students can try an unlimited number of drafts, different versions, or new approaches, until they are satisfied with the result.

Another option is to collect and review student portfolios periodically, giving a grade for progress and quality at each review. Some teachers use a midterm and a final portfolio, concentrating the grade to between 66–75 percent on the final collection to maintain the emphasis on revision. Others choose to review portfolios three times during the term, once for progress, once for a preliminary grade determination, and once for final analysis.

Still other instructors employ a configuration that combines traditional grading with the portfolio concept. You might, for example, collect essays and give grades as usual, making sure to make comments directed toward the student's pending revision. Then students can rework these graded essays throughout the term for inclusion in their final portfolio, which will be reviewed for a final cumulative grade and averaged with their other term grades, similar to a final exam.

Whatever method is employed, successful instructors mold the style of portfolio writing to their own strengths and teaching styles as well as to their particular situations. The teacher with one hundred students per term cannot possibly do traditional grading and then tack on an additional element of portfolio grading if he or she intends to maintain any level of sanity. On the other hand, a teacher with one composition class might want to try using a number of individual conferences throughout the term, one or two preliminary portfolio reviews, and a culminating final portfolio. Assess your techniques and teaching conditions carefully and honestly, then design a configuration appropriate to those constraints.

When introducing a portfolio system, keep the following potential pitfalls in mind.

1. *Avoid grading your own work.* Too often, through well-meaning comments and directions, a teacher can appropriate a student's paper. Looking at too many drafts and making too many detailed comments makes the student dependent and stifles independent critical thinking. The student is then writing to achieve the teacher's vision of the paper, not his or her own. If a final portfolio reflects the teacher's expertise rather than the student's, the system is not working well. Questions ("What experience can you share to support this point?") and reader response comments ("At this point, I wasn't sure how these two paragraphs related") can be the most helpful in guiding students and avoiding this problem.

2. *Avoid grading **another** student's work.* As in any composition classroom, the portfolio class offers many opportunities for a student to get inappropriate help from others. A certain amount of in-class writing, of individual conferencing, and of requiring and checking multiple drafts will help minimize this problem.

3. *Expect and learn to manage student grade anxiety.* Students may worry greatly if their final evaluation will be satisfactory when they are not receiving periodic grades. On the other hand, some

students may have an inflated idea of the quality of their work if they do not receive some early evaluation. Providing some method of early progress/quality assessment will help them understand where they stand in relationship to your standards. Such a preliminary assessment can be anything from an informal conference ending in a joint teacher/student determination of a grade and suggestions for improvement (a grade which is not recorded since every item is subject to revision) to a formal teacher-generated score that counts toward the term grade.

4. *Avoid increasing your workload.* While portfolio grading is not a way to cut back those lengthy hours of reading student work, it need not add to your hours either. Remember that when you are looking at multiple drafts, you need not make as many comments on each. Pointing out one paragraph that needs a topic sentence, for example, and suggesting others can benefit from the same revision, helps the student review essays independently; such instruction may lead to improved learning since the student is not dependent on your comments. Highlighting one or two comma splices and suggesting the student look for other mistakes of this kind can have the same result. Also, since the student is going to go back and rework these papers, you need not comment on issues you have not yet addressed in class. You can concentrate on single issues on each draft, a practice that will make both your job and the student's job more targeted and effective, less fragmented and frustrating.

5. *Avoid procrastination.* Some students might be inclined to hand in less carefully done work on early drafts when they know only the final product "counts." If you allow this to happen, you are either doing the student's revision work by reading and commenting or wasting your efforts before he or she has really put enough thinking or writing into the project. To avoid this problem, many instructors give appropriate credit for early drafts, encouraging students to present their best work at each stage.

Teacher procrastination is another possibility. Although the temptation might be to wait to look at papers carefully until the end of the term, only spot-checking early drafts, the quality of the final portfolios will be directly related to early and continuous guidance. Lengthy review and comments on the final collection might be interesting to some students, but will not be particularly instructive and will keep you working until the last minute before grades are due. One of the best ways to assign a final grade to the portfolio is to schedule individual conferences (these can be done in 15–20 minutes) in which the student reviews the portfolio with you and, together, you assess improvements, remaining weaknesses, and overall quality of the pieces in the collection, taking time to point out particularly strong revisions you have noted in several of the essays.

Implemented thoughtfully and individually, portfolio writing/grading can be very rewarding. For students, it can be a step toward more intrinsic motivation and greater independence as writers. For the instructor, it is a way to reflect a more realistic notion of the way good writing *really* happens—through a continual process of revision—and the portfolio can provide a better opportunity to observe and acknowledge substantive change in students' skills and habits.

Part 1
The Basics of the Short Essay

Chapter 1
Prewriting, p. 3

■ Summary

Getting Started (or Soup-Can Labels Can Be Fascinating)
- you have some valuable ideas to tell your reader
- you want to communicate those ideas to your reader

Selecting a Subject
- start early
- find your best space
- select something in which you currently have a strong interest
- narrow a large subject

Finding Your Essay's Purpose and Focus

Pump-Primer Techniques
- listing
- freewriting
- looping
- the boomerang
- clustering
- cubing
- interviewing
- the cross-examination
- sketching
- dramatizing the subject

After You've Found Your Focus

Practicing What You've Learned

Assignment

Discovering Your Audience

How to Identify Your Readers
- determine who the audience is for your assignment
- if a specific audience is designated, determine its reasons for reading
- determine what knowledge your audience has of your subject
- determine your audience's attitudes
- determine special qualities your audience might have
  - Readers don't like to be bored.
  - They hate confusion and disorder.
  - They want to think and learn.
  - They want to see and feel what you see and feel.
  - They are turned off by pretentious, phony voices.

15

Practicing What You've Learned

Assignment

Keeping a Journal

- confront your fears of writing; conquer the blank page
- improve your powers of observation
- save your brilliant ideas
- save other people's brilliant ideas
- be creative
- prepare for class
- record responses to class discussions
- focus on a problem
- practice audience awareness
- describe your own writing process
- write a progress report
- increase sensitivity to language
- write your own textbook

■ Answers to "Practicing What You've Learned" Exercises

Practicing What You've Learned, p. 18

A. 1. This subject is far too broad. It might be narrowed by defining the university's role in a specific field, such as researching solar energy for use in homes.
   2. This subject could be adequately treated in a short essay.
   3. Because of the number of Shakespearean characters, this subject is too large. It might be narrowed to one or two characters of one play.
   4. Obviously, this subject covers too much ground.
   5. A short paper might give a satisfactory overview of this hobby, but for a better essay the student might focus on some specific aspect, such as "how to find rare/older cards," "how to assess the value of a baseball card," or "types of baseball cards."
   6. This subject could be discussed in a short essay, though again the student might profit from focusing on some specific aspect or particular kind of gun control laws—the state/city they govern.
   7. The most serious disadvantages would be covered in a short paper.
   8. The various models and functions of computers are a complex subject, too broad for a brief essay.
   9. This subject could be described adequately.
   10. Once the subject is narrowed to a specific type of bike (e.g., mountain, road, touring), selecting a bicycle would be a good topic for a process paper.

B. You will, of course, receive a variety of suitable answers here. Be sure that the students narrow the subjects sufficiently instead of stopping halfway. For example, a student might be tempted to narrow "music" to "rock music" or "education" to "college," but these subjects are still too broad for a short essay. Better answers will be more specific: "music" to "Melissa Etheridge's latest album," "education" to "required courses," etc. If done properly, this exercise should show students that selecting and narrowing a subject is the first step to discovering the main purpose of their essays. Once this step is mastered, students should find that formulating a thesis is not the difficult problem they might have imagined.

16

Practicing What You've Learned, p. 22

A. Responses to Geico ad:

1. The Geico ad appeals to an older audience: middle-aged males and females who were teenagers and young adults in the 1960s. The ad reaches across social and economic class boundaries and connects to audiences on a emotional, nostalgic level.

2. This audience may still be interested in the same types of activism and causes they embraced in their youth and the natural imagery in the background of the ad may resonate with the audience's "free spirit." As aging members of society, and nearing retirement, this audience is also concerned with making smart financial decisions, and would, therefore, appreciate Geico's "Special Treatment" and good value.

3. Geico "rewards" customers who "survived" the wild '60s. This may evoke feelings of camaraderie and understanding between the customer and the company, which creates a strong emotional appeal. The "experienced driver discounts" and claims of "Average savings $500" also appeal to a more mature, value-conscious customer.

4. The phrase "Survive the '60s? You deserve special treatment" strongly resonates with the target audience.

B. Answers will vary.

Discussion of Assignment, p. 23

A. The radio audience will want details about the supposed benefits of Breatharianism, even though the students may be skeptical and probably think Brooks is a phony. Including some comments like "Sure, I know you are probably skeptical" **may** show audience awareness and may make the ad more believable.

The parade permit application would try to show that these people would not pose a threat to public order. Moreover, this might lead to more business for the community as well as a sense that the town was interested in the health and welfare of its citizens and even the environment.

In the report, details like a nutritional study showing the bad effects this diet would have on health, a record of Brooks's activity in other states and cities, and some personal testimony from other former Breatharians all would strengthen the case. Students will need to remember to do more than just say, "He's obviously guilty; let's leave it at that!"

B. *Collaborative Activity, p. 25*
Answers will vary.

Chapter 2
The Thesis Statement, p. 31

■ Summary

What Is a Thesis? What Does a "Working Thesis" Do?

Can a "Working Thesis" Change?

Guidelines for Writing a Good Thesis

- state the writer's clearly defined opinion on some subject
- assert one main idea
- have something worthwhile to say
- limit thesis to fit the assignment
- state thesis clearly in specific terms
- state thesis clearly, often in first or second paragraph

Avoiding Common Errors in Thesis Statements

- don't merely announce or describe your intentions; do state an attitude
- don't clutter a thesis with expressions like "In my opinion"; do be forceful, speak directly and with conviction
- don't be unreasonable or insulting; do avoid irresponsible charges, name calling, and profanity
- don't merely state a fact or idea that is self-evident or dead-ended
- don't express a thesis in the form of a question

Practicing What You've Learned

Assignment

Using the Essay Map
Practicing What You've Learned

Assignment

■ Answers to "Practicing What You've Learned" Exercises

Practicing What You've Learned, p. 39

A. 1. Inadequate. It is unnecessary to say "I think," and "interesting" is too broad to have much meaning. What is it about the movie that is interesting—the subject, the acting, the cinematography? A good thesis is more specific.
   2. Inadequate. First, a thesis should be expressed in a declarative sentence, not in a question. Second, comparing Japanese automobiles to American automobiles is too broad.
   3. Inadequate. This is merely a statement that "some people" have this opinion. The purpose of a paper on this subject, however, is to reveal and support the author's opinion. Moreover "bad" is simply too subjective, not specific; still, it does provide for the heuristic question "In which ways?"

4. Inadequate. "My essay will tell you" is an announcement.
5. Adequate. This specific assertion will lead to a discussion of the reasons why final examinations should be given before the winter break.
6. Inadequate. It is not necessary to mention that the tuition increase will be a "terrible" burden. This thesis also has two parts that need to be separated: what, exactly, the extra burden of a tuition increase is, and what that has to do with the quality of education.
7. Inadequate. The writer's point is unclear. Does she believe body piercing should be illegal, or is it merely unsightly? It is also unclear whether the writer is unable to look people in the face who are "into body piercing" or if she finds facial piercing particularly offensive.
8. Inadequate. This statement is unreasonable in its claim.
9. Adequate.
10. Inadequate. The phrase "very important" is too vague. The thesis should assert a specific idea, such as "Having a close friend you can talk to makes adjusting to dorm living a lot easier."

B. These weak or faulty theses may be rewritten in a variety of ways; the comments below are intended to help you identify the problem with each example.

1. "Negative experience" is too broad; students should substitute specific descriptions.
2. This is a "so what?" thesis. Students should either take a stand on the issue or state why it is important for the reader to know the advantages and disadvantages.
3. "One big headache" is too vague.
4. Students should omit the phrase "In this paper I will debate." Also, the writer's position should be clear.
5. Too vague. What is it we need to do about billboard clutter?
6. What is missing from this thesis statement is a purpose. Why do the insurance laws need to be rewritten? Which laws?
7. Too vague. In what ways is it good for the rider?
8. "In my opinion" can be deleted, and "fantastic" is too vague.
9. Too broad. What effects did the Civil Rights movement have? Were they positive or negative? Both?
10. This thesis lacks a clear, single focus/purpose. Does the writer want to discuss the band's merits or its venue selection choices?

Practicing What You've Learned, p. 42

A. 1. because of its . . . innovative editing.
2. Such a move . . . highway maintenance.
3. To guarantee . . . personalized design
4. because it's . . . more luxurious.
5. To qualify . . . and training.
6. Through . . . squads
7. Because . . . fatty tissue
8. deductions . . . will be taxed.
9. They're . . . fun to grow.
10. His spirit of protest . . . arrangements

B. Student responses will vary.

C. Student responses will vary.

Discussion of Assignment, p. 43

Many of these quotations lend themselves to essays developed by example or narration, and teachers may wish to use one of them as an assignment prompt when those methods of essay development are being studied. Some of these topics would also make excellent prompts for an in-class "response" essay assignment (see Chapter 15).

Chapter 3
The Body Paragraphs, p. 47

■ Summary

Planning the Body of Your Essay

Composing the Body Paragraphs

The Topic Sentence
- supports the thesis by clearly stating a main point in the discussion
- announces what the paragraph will be about
- controls the subject matter of the paragraph

Focusing Your Topic Sentence

Placing Your Topic Sentence

Practicing What You've Learned

Assignment

Applying What You've Learned to Your Writing

Paragraph Development
- include enough supporting information or evidence to make readers understand the topic sentence
- make the information clear and specific
- avoid vague generalities and repetitious ideas

Paragraph Length
- long enough to accomplish its purpose and short enough to be interesting
- avoid the one- or two-sentence paragraph
- divide longish paragraphs at a logical point; use transitional phrases

Practicing What You've Learned

Assignment

Applying What You've Learned to Your Writing

Paragraph Unity
- stick to the subject
- unify sentences around a central or main idea—topic sentence
- unify paragraphs around thesis

Practicing What You've Learned

Applying What You've Learned to Your Writing

Paragraph Coherence

- use a recognizable order of information
- order of time
- order of space
- deductive order
- inductive order
- use transitional words and phrases
- examples
- comparison/contrast
- sequence
- results
- repeat key words
- substitute pronouns for key nouns
- use parallelism
- use a variety of transitional devices
- avoid whiplash—maintain coherence

Practicing What You've Learned

Paragraph Sequence

- consider logic, effect

Transitions between Paragraphs

- use to link paragraphs, ideas
- vary the type and placement to avoid sounding mechanical and boring

Applying What You've Learned to Your Writing

■ Answers to "Practicing What You've Learned" Exercises

Practicing What You've Learned, p. 55

A. 1. Denim is one of America's . . .
    2. Adlai Stevenson, American statesman . . . The last sentence belongs in another paragraph as it does not illustrate Stevenson's wit.
    3. . . . almost every wedding tradition . . . Weddings may vary . . . (concluding sentence)
    4. If any of these sound familiar, . . .
    5. In actuality, the most popular instrument . . .
    6. The wonderful tradition . . .

B. Answers will vary.

C. Your students should add topic sentences that resemble the following:

    1. Some highly successful people were not recognized as brilliant thinkers in their youth.
    2. Most of the inexpensive trinkets sold when Elvis Presley was a popular rock star have now become much more valuable.
    3. While an author's book or play may be respected by the public, the writer in person often receives little appreciation.
    4. Although we tend to think of "record seasons" in terms of victorious teams, losing seasons are also permanently recorded in the annals of football.

D. Student responses will vary.

Practicing What You've Learned, p. 63

A. 1. The extremely vague adjectives (best, interesting, concerned, great) are the first clue that this paragraph is unfocused. The paragraph might target one of Wilson's strengths, then explain and illustrate it. Also, the reader-oriented purpose of this paragraph is puzzling.
   2. These are generalized complaints about advice columns are repetitious and move in several directions. The solution is to focus on one idea and then use examples to support this assertion.
   3. This is another general survey of the topic that needs more concrete development to make it more coherent and tie it more closely to the topic sentence.
   4. The topic sentence here—"Nursing homes are often sad places"—says it all. The rest of the paragraph is merely a repetition of that fact in different words.
   5. While the writer has a clear distinction in mind between acquaintances and friends, trite and overused generalities ("being close to you," "sharing intimate things," "happy about being alive") add no real development to the paragraph. Also, using "you" in the hypothetical examples is ineffective; detailed, real, personal, or observed examples would be much more compelling.

B. Answers will vary.

Assignment, p. 65

A. Answers will vary.
B. Answers will vary.
C. Answers will vary.

Practicing What You've Learned, p. 67

Delete the following sentences from the sample paragraphs:

1. During this period, songwriters . . .
2. Another well-known incident of cannibalism in the West occurred . . .
3. To publicize his new product . . . (Some readers might also consider the last sentence a break, though it might be seen as additional information to conclude the paragraph.)
4. U.S. Representative from Colorado . . . (to end of paragraph)
5. This example illustrates a drift from the original topic (dorm living providing a good way to meet people) into a new, slightly different topic (new friends teach students about other countries…hope to visit). The writer might use the friend from Peru as an example of her original position, but overall she needs to rewrite the last half of her paragraph to bring it in line with her topic sentence.

Practicing What You've Learned, p. 74

A. The first paragraph, on the apartment, is ordered by space, with the point of view moving from the left of the front door to the back of the room to the right of the door.

   The second paragraph, on acts of greeting, is ordered chronologically, with details selected from the seventeenth-century tip through today.

   The third paragraph, on exams, is ordered by parallelism, with sentences structured in the repeated pattern of "synonym for students + verb."

B. The transitional devices in each paragraph are underlined:

   1. Each year I follow a system when preparing firewood to use in my stove. <u>First</u>, I hike about a mile from my house with my bow saw in hand. I <u>then</u> select three good size oak trees and mark them with orange ties. <u>Next</u>, I saw through the base of each <u>tree</u> about two feet from the ground. <u>After</u> I fell the <u>trees, not only</u> do I trim away the branches, <u>but</u> I <u>also</u> sort the scrap from the usable limbs. I find cutting the <u>trees</u> into manageable length logs is too much for one day;

however, I roll them off the ground so they will not begin to rot. The next day I cut the trees into eight-foot lengths, which allows me to handle them more easily. Once they are cut, I roll them along the fire lane to the edge of the road where I stack them neatly but not too high. The next day I borrow my uncle's van, drive to the pile of logs, and load as many logs as I can, thus reducing the number of trips. When I finally have all the logs in my backyard, I begin sawing them into eighteen-inch lengths. I create large piles that consequently have to be split and finally stacked. The logs will age and dry until winter when I will make daily trips to the woodpile.

2. Fans of professional baseball and football argue continually over which is America's favorite spectator sport. Though the figures on attendance for each vary with every new season, certain arguments remain the same, spelling out both the enduring appeals of each game and something about the people who love to watch. Football, for instance, is a quicker, more physical sport, and football fans enjoy the emotional involvement they feel while watching. Baseball, on the other hand, seems more mental, like chess, and attracts those fans who prefer a quieter, more complicated game. In addition, professional football teams usually play no more than sixteen games a season, providing fans with a whole week between games to work themselves up to a pitch of excitement and expectation. Baseball teams, however, play almost every day for six months, so that the typical baseball fan is not so crushed by missing a game, knowing there will be many other chances to attend. Finally football fans seem to love the halftime pageantry, the marching bands, and the pretty cheerleaders, whereas baseball fans are more content to concentrate on the game's finer details and spend the breaks between innings filling out their own private scorecards.

C. The choice of transition words may vary slightly from student to student, but here is a typical response to the dinosaur paragraph:

dinosaurs, then, Because, reptiles, however, although, dinosaurs, they, as well as, Another, dinosaurs, In addition, dinosaurs, also, dinosaurs, therefore, creatures, other, scientists, dinosaurs, or.

D. The sentences in paragraph 1 should be grouped in this order: G, H, B, F, D, A, C, E.

E. Student responses will vary.

Chapter 4
Beginnings and Endings, p. 81

■ Summary

How to Write a Good Lead-in

- a paradoxical or intriguing statement
- an arresting statistic or shocking statement
- a question
- a quotation or literary allusion
- a relevant story, joke, or anecdote
- a description, often used for emotional appeal
- a factual statement or summary who-what-where-when-why lead-in
- an analogy or comparison
- a contrast or before-and-after scenario
- a personal experience
- a catalog of relevant examples or facts
- a statement of a problem or a popular misconception
- a brief dialogue to introduce the topic
- a proverb, maxim, or motto
- a recognition, revelation, or insight
- an appeal to a common or imagined experience

Avoiding Errors in Lead-ins

- make sure your lead-in introduces your thesis
- keep lead-in brief
- don't begin with an apology or complaint
- don't assume your audience already knows your subject matter
- stay clear of overused lead-ins

Practicing What You've Learned

Assignment

How to Write a Good Concluding Paragraph

- a restatement of both the thesis and the essay's major points
- an evaluation of the importance of the essay's subject
- a statement of the essay's broader implications
- a recommendation or call to action
- a warning based on the essay's thesis
- a quotation that emphasizes or sums up the point of the essay
- an anecdote or brief example that emphasizes or sums up the point of the essay
- an ironic twist, witticism, pun or playful use of words
- an image or description that lends finality to the essay

- a rhetorical question that makes the reader think about the essay's main point
- a forecast based on the essay's thesis
- a return to a technique used in your lead-in

Avoiding Errors in Conclusions
- avoid a mechanical ending
- don't introduce new points
- don't tack on a conclusion
- don't change your stance
- avoid trite expressions
- don't insult or anger your reader

Practicing What You've Learned

Assignment

How to Write a Good Title
- attracts readers' interest
- announces the tone of the essay
- suggests content
- is not underlined or put in quotation marks
- is capitalized according to MLA guidelines
- clarifies scope and/or tone of essay

Practicing What You've Learned

Assignment

Applying What You've Learned to Your Writing

■ Answers to "Practicing What You've Learned" Exercises

Practicing What You've Learned, p. 85

1. uses a quotation from a philosopher
2. uses questions and a factual statement
3. uses an arresting statistic
4. sets up a before/after contrast through a personal experience
5. uses a factual description of an event and an intriguing statement.

Assignment, p. 86

A. Answers will vary.
B. Answers will vary.

Practicing What You've Learned, p. 90

Example number one is too mechanical and should not use words such as "My thesis in this essay stated." Number two simply drops in the quotation without connecting it to the discussion, relies on clichés ("long hard road") , drifts off subject (from going back to school to questioning value of certain courses), and finally ends weakly ("maybe it would be for others"). Example number three will insult many readers or at least annoy them with its "either-or" exaggerated claim.

Assignment, p. 91

Answers will vary.

Practicing What You've Learned, p. 92

Most of these titles are bland and lack information that would attract readers. Students' answers will vary, but they should be encouraged to add a point of view and specific words; labels and words such as "Essay Assignment" and "My Interpretation" should be deleted and replaced with focused titles that suggest content and set the appropriate tone.

Examples:

1. Advice for College Freshman…Needs a specific focus and clarity to interest the appropriate audience. (What sort of advice? What specific area—academic? social? campus life? What kind of college? Traditional or nontraditional students?)

2. Essay Assignment #3: Review of a Favorite Movie…Replace this label with a title that presents the movie's name (or a recognizable part of it) and indicates the overall assessment of the film; this title may also provide an opportunity for students to use word play or a witty title, depending on the tone of the essay and movie's content (e.g., *Cinematic Riches in Millionaire*, page 514 in Chapter 18).

Assignment, p. 92

A. Answers will vary.
B. Answers will vary.

Chapter 5
Drafting and Revising: Creative Thinking, Critical Thinking, p. 95

■ Summary

What Is Revision?
- revision is a thinking process

When Does Revision Occur?
- revision occurs throughout the writing process

Myths about Revision
- revision is not autopsy
- revision is not limited to editing or proofreading
- revision is not punishment or busywork

Can I Learn to Improve My Revision Skills?

Preparing to Draft: Some Time-Saving Hints
- if handwriting drafts, use only one side of the paper
- leave big margins on both sides of each page for additional information
- devise a system of symbols to remind you of changes you want to make later
- leave blank spots to note areas needing further development
- use a line or x for corrections or potential deletions; don't scratch out original material completely
- try to work from a typed copy
- always keep notes, outlines, drafts, and an extra copy of your final paper

Writing with Computers
- save your work regularly and print a copy of every draft
- learn to use the editing tools of your software, but don't rely on spell-checkers
- use the search command to sweep for commonly made errors
- read printed versions of your text to see what your readers will see

Writing Centers, Computer Labs, and Electronic Networks

A Revision Process for Your Drafts

I. Revising for Purpose, Thesis, and Audience
- fulfill assignment objectives
- follow directions carefully
- understand the purpose of your essay
- comprehend your audience—put a face to it
- select appropriate strategies for your goal

II. Revising for Ideas and Evidence
- relate major points to thesis
- focus a position
- use effective and relevant points
- state and locate points clearly

What Is Critical Thinking?
- the ability to analyze and evaluate your own ideas and those of others

Thinking Critically as a Writer
- learn to distinguish fact from opinion
- support your own opinions with evidence
- evaluate the strength of your evidence
- use enough specific supporting evidence
- watch for biases and strong emotions that may undermine evidence
- check evidence for logical fallacies

III. Revising for Organization
- use an appropriate strategy for your purpose
- order points logically
- use clear topic sentences
- use transitions between paragraphs
- proportion ideas for effectiveness
- use an effective title and lead-in
- conclude thoughtfully, emphatically, or memorably
- don't be hesitant to restructure drafts

IV. Revising for Clarity and Style
- check for clear, precise sentences
- avoid wordiness
- provide a variety of sentence lengths
- check for appropriate word choices
- use active verbs and lively language
- eliminate jargon, clichés, and pretentious language
- use an authentic voice

V. Editing for Errors
- read aloud
- know your enemies/your own weaknesses in punctuation/grammar
- read backwards
- learn some "tricks" for punctuation/grammar problems
- eliminate diction and mechanical errors readers find annoying
- use your tools (reference texts such as dictionary, thesaurus, handbook)

VI. Proofreading
- set work aside for a time; review with "fresh eyes"
- freshen pages for a "professional look"

A Final Checklist for Your Essay
Practicing What You've Learned

Collaborative Activities: Group Work, Peer Revision Workshops, and Team Projects Benefiting from Revision Workshops

As writer:
- develop a constructive attitude
- come prepared
- evaluate suggestions carefully
- find the good in bad advice

As reader:
- develop a constructive attitude
- be clear and specific
- address important issues
- encourage the writer
- understand your role as a critical reader

Practicing What You've Learned

Assignment

Some Last Advice: How to Play with Your Mental Blocks

- give yourself as much time as possible to write your essay
- verbalize ideas
- break paper into manageable bits
- get the juices flowing and the pen moving
- set reasonable limits of time for writing to prevent anxiety
- give yourself permission to write garbage
- warm up by writing something easier
- imagine writing to a friend
- remember that writer's block is temporary
- if you have a bright idea for one section, move to it or jot it down
- reconnect with your subject matter
- do something else for a while
- relax, and remember that no one writes perfectly every time

■ Answers to "Practicing What You've Learned" Exercises

Practicing What You've Learned, p. 111

A. Answers will vary.

B. **"Maybe You Shouldn't Go Away to College"**

This student needs help with organization, paragraph development and unity, and sentence construction. The comparison of the local school to the out-of-town school should be made much clearer in each body paragraph through the addition of specific examples.

Paragraph 1: The thesis is clear but the essay map is expressed awkwardly.

Paragraph 2: The contrast between the cost of attending an out-of-town college and living at home needs a clearer statement in the topic sentence. How can the writer know that out-of-town colleges always have higher tuition? Perhaps it would be more effective to discuss the expense of transportation rather than tuition, which varies from school to school regardless of location. The example of room and board should be developed further.

Paragraph 3: This sentence seems off the subject; omit the paragraph.

Paragraph 4: This paragraph does have a point, but the writer needs to focus and clarify what kinds of "changes" she means. Development of the paragraph should be improved by adding some specific examples of the pressures and changes involved in going away to college; the writer could then show how the security of home could make such changes easier.

Paragraphs 5 and 6: These two paragraphs discuss the same point and therefore need to be combined. However, instead of merely asking whether students should be forced to break away at this time, the writer should persuasively argue her own position, perhaps by explaining some of the responsibilities of going away to college. (She also needs to make sure that her discussion of "responsibilities" does not merely repeat the discussion of "pressures" in paragraph 4. Are these two points really different? If they aren't, her essay map also needs rethinking.)

Paragraph 7: The conclusion is unnecessarily brief, although the writer does try to end with a play on words ("right road" and "just around the corner").

C.   Possible Answer: One of the most interesting books I've read lately is *Bold Spirit*, by Linda Lawrence Hunt. It is the true story of Hega Estby's 1896 walk across America, from eastern Washington to New York City, to win a $10,000 prize to save the family farm. Accompanied by her teenage daughter Clara, the two set out with only five dollars each and walked 5000 miles on foot while dressed in Victorian clothing, despite severe bad weather and dangerous encounters along the way. Helga and her daughter arrived safely in New York, but, unfortunately, they were unable to collect their prize money. Afterwards, Helga's family was so embarrassed by her walk that they burned her diary, notes, and newspaper clippings. The story was forgotten for many years, but was recently revived by Helga's daughter-in-law, who had secretly saved an album of clippings from the fire.

Assignment, p. 114

Answers will vary.

Practicing What You've Learned, p. 120

Collaborative Activity: Letter to Mom and Dad

This activity is included to help students think about revision in larger ways, not just as proofreading for small surface errors. It's also designed to introduce some humor into the classroom and might be used to offset some of the stress students could be feeling about revising their own drafts. Clearly, Bubba is being duped by his girlfriend and her so-called "brother" who are trying to con him with the sick grandmother story; he obviously has other problems as well (his roommate, car wreck, rash, and fight). Students should be encouraged to have fun helping poor Bubba figure out better ways to ask his parents for money; they might start by explaining to Bubba the importance of "audience awareness" (discussed in Chapter 1) and the need for a clearly stated main point (Chapter 2), as well as the selection of pertinent, persuasive details (Chapter 3). This exercise also underscores the necessity of cutting out any details that might be damaging to one's purpose!

Assignment, p. 121

Answers will vary.

Chapter 6
Effective Sentences, p. 125

■ Summary

Developing a Clear Style

- give your sentences content
- make your sentences specific
- avoid overpacking your sentences
- fix fragments
- pay attention to word order
- avoid mixed constructions and faulty predication

Practicing What You've Learned

Developing a Concise Style

- avoid deadwood constructions
- avoid redundancy
- carefully consider your passive verbs
- avoid pretentiousness

Practicing What You've Learned

Assignment

Developing a Lively Style

- use specific, descriptive verbs
- use specific, precise modifiers that help the reader see, hear, or feel what you are describing
- emphasize people when possible
- vary your sentence style
- avoid overuse of any one kind of construction in the same sentence
- don't change your point of view between or within sentences

Practicing What You've Learned

Assignment

Developing an Emphatic Style

- word order
- coordination
- subordination

Practicing What You've Learned

Assignment

Applying What You've Learned to Your Writing

■ Answers to "Practicing What You've Learned" Exercises

Practicing What You've Learned, p. 134

Some suggestions follow:

A. 1. According to *TV Guide*, the new detective show on TV stars Phil Noir and is set in the 1940s.
2. Roger's marketing skills made him important to his company's sales department. I can't help but wonder if he is welcome.
3. *Biofeedback: How to Stop It* has so many funny and sarcastic comments about California self-help fads, I couldn't put it down.
4. The magician became disillusioned when his assistant stole the disappearing rabbit, the magic wand, and the invisible ink.
5. Are you afraid poor auto repair service will ruin your next road trip? Come to the Fix-It Shop for expert care; we'll replace worn parts on your car for your peace of mind.
6. At my local college, I've signed up for a class in "Cultivating Mold in Your Refrigerator for Fun and Profit."
7. Lois Mueller, the author of *The Underachiever's Guide to Very Small Business Opportunities* and *Whine Your Way to Success,* is having an autograph party at the campus bookstore today at noon.
8. Some people find reading their horoscopes insightful or entertaining; others find it a waste of time.
9. Upon being asked if she would like to live forever, one contestant in the 1994 Miss USA contest replied that she would if she could, but she can't.

B. 1. Go to the police to learn ways to avoid being accosted in the subway.
2. Escorted down the aisle by her father, the bride wore an antique wedding gown—a family heirloom.
3. I miss my dog even though she has been dead almost five years now.
4. For sale: Unique handmade gifts for that special, hard-to-shop-for person in your life.
5. After putting off surgery for years, I finally had my leg operated on during Thanksgiving break.
6. We need to hire two nonsmoking teachers for the preschool class of three-year-olds.
7. The story of Rip Van Winkle illustrates the dangers of oversleeping.
8. We gave our waterbed to our friends.
9. Neither people who are allergic to chocolate nor children under six should be given the new vaccine.
10. "I remember a meeting in the Oval Office with a mother whose child was abducted by the North Koreans."

Practicing What You've Learned, p. 139

1. He lost the editing job because of his careless and sloppy proofreading.
2. Staff members noted that many employees and their families at the company picnic threw their trash on the ground.
3. My older brother Austin can't drive to work this week because he wrecked his car early Saturday morning.
4. Today, we often criticize advertising that demeans women or represents them unfairly.
5. The twin brothers' defense attorney objected to the prosecutor's attempt to introduce the antique gun.
6. In "Now Is the Winter of Our Discount Tent," the poet expresses her disgust with camping.
7. Although the boss appeared to be listening, we didn't think she took our concerns seriously.
8. Learning word processing makes you more efficient at work, school, and home.

9. Some people assert their superiority by being rude to restaurant servers.

10. To improve my chances for promotion, I decided to propose to the boss's daughter.

Assignment, p. 140

Answers will vary.

Practicing What You've Learned, p. 144

A. 1. After listening to the whining moan of the reactor, I'm not sure that nuclear power has a future.
   2. The City Council members were embarrassed because the application forms for grants were mailed without stamps.
   3. Watching Jim Bob eat pork chops was nauseating.
   4. For sale: elegant antique bureau with thick legs and extra-large side handles.
   5. We want everyone to have fun.
   6. My roommate may be eccentric but he's loyal to his friends.
   7. After reading "The Looter's Guide to Riot-Prone Cities," Eddie requested an immediate transfer.
   8. The wild oats soup was so delicious we slurped it all down in five minutes.
   9. Warren Peace threw kitty litter in the air when his cat, Chairman Meow, won first place in the pet show.
   10. The new diet gave me headaches and leg cramps.

Assignment, p. 144

A. Answers will vary depending upon the samples students address. This assignment can easily become an in-class, small group activity, as students discuss and select the Most Lifeless Prose winner.

B. Again, student responses will vary. The activity encourages clarity and conciseness but may also allow students to practice figurative language, word play, and audience awareness.

Examples:

Join the Campus Chess Club! New partners offer new challenges! Come to our Open House on…

Thinking about your next move? Pick up the Campus Housing Department's new brochure…

Yes, we admit your dog is incredibly smart…but remember the Library does not permit entry to any pets other than service animals!

Practicing What You've Learned, p. 149

A. 1. Joe Louis, one-time heavyweight boxing champion, once said, "I don't really like money but it quiets my nerves."
   2. Recent polls suggest that most Americans get their news from television.
   3. Hunger is the most urgent of all the world's problems.
   4. Of all the foreign countries I visited last year, my favorite was Greece.
   5. One habit I will not tolerate is knuckle-cracking.

B. 1. The guru rejected his dentist's offer of Novocain because he could transcend dental medication.
   2. Because John incorrectly identified Harper Lee as the author of the south-of-the-border classic *Tequila Mockingbird,* he failed his literature test.
   3. She pressed "9" but when she couldn't find an "11" on the dial, Peggy Sue's house burned.
   4. Although the police had only a few clues, they suspected that Jean and David had strangled each other in a desperate struggle over control of the thermostat.

34

5. Described by one critic as a "pinhead chiller," *Sorority Babes in the Slimeball Bowl-o-rama* (1988) is Bubba's favorite movie.

6. Because their menu includes banana split personality, repressed duck, shrimp basket case, and self-expresso, we're going to the Psychoanalysis Restaurant.

7. Kato lost the junior high spelling bee when he couldn't spell *DNA*.

8. Colorado hosts an annual BobFest to honor all persons named Bob, and events include playing softbob, bobbing for apples, listening to bob-pipes, and eating bob-e-que.

9. When the earthquake shook the city, Louise was performing primal-scream therapy. (Or: Because Louise was performing primal-scream therapy, an earthquake shook the city!)

10. In 1789 many Parisians bought a new perfume called "Guillotine" because they wanted to be on the cutting edge of fashion.

C. Obviously, the sentences may be combined in many ways. Here are some examples.

1. While living on a raft on the Mississippi River, a runaway boy, accompanied by an escaped slave, has many adventures and learns valuable lessons about friendship and human kindness.

2. A young man returning from prison joins his family in their move from the Dust Bowl to California, where they find intolerance and dishonest employers instead of jobs.

3. A mad scientist who wants to re-create life makes a gruesome monster in his laboratory but is killed by his rebellious creature as the villagers, in revolt, storm the castle.

Assignment, p. 150

A. Answers will vary.

B. Student responses will vary, but here are two samples:

1. A new product called a "dieter's conscience," a small recorder installed inside your refrigerator, reminds you to eat less. When you open the refrigerator door, a voice says, "You eating again? No wonder you're getting fat. Close the door; it's getting warm" and then bursts into insane laughter—all designed to encourage you to rethink your eating habits.

2. The "Talking Tombstone" is another new product, produced by the Gone-But-Not-Forgotten Company of Burbank, California. Anyone walking near the tombstone activates a recording made by the departed before death. Volume is controlled by body heat: the closer someone is to the grave, the louder the voice. Messages may be personalized; a hypochondriac, for instance, might want to joke, "See, I told you I was sick!" Such a device may change the way we think about cemeteries.

Chapter 7
Word Logic, p. 153

■ Summary

Selecting the Correct Words

Accuracy

- confused words
- idiomatic phrases

Levels of Language

- colloquial
- informal
- formal

Tone

- invective
- sarcasm
- irony
- flippancy or cuteness
- sentimentality
- preachiness
- pomposity

Connotation and Denotation

- emotional association versus literal meaning

Practicing What You've Learned

Selecting the Best Words

- make them as precise as possible
- make them as fresh and original as possible
- don't use trendy expressions or slang
- use texting or Internet language appropriately
- select simple, direct words your readers can easily understand
- call things by their proper names
- avoid sexist language
- enliven your writing with figurative language when appropriate
- vary your word choice so that your prose does not sound wordy, repetitious, or monotonous
- remember that wordiness is a major problem for all writers, even professionals

Practicing What You've Learned

Assignment

Applying What You've Learned to Your Writing

■ Answers to "Practicing What You've Learned" Exercises

Practicing What You've Learned, p. 159

A. 1. two weeks, two friends, too short, too tired, you're, too broke
   2. who's, photographic, accepted, number, compliments
   3. It's, too, their, generic, they're, rolls, your
   4. foul
   5. regardless, course, vain
   6. Ants
   7. lose, your, metal, its
   8. council, affect

B. 1. The sunset signaled the cat to come out for its nightly prowl.
   2. "You're fired" may tempt students, but it, too, seems unreasonable. Ask them to consider other options such as "We no longer require your services, thank you."
   3. I wanted information about the poor.
   4. If the bill to legalize marijuana is passed, we think most Americans will soon be smoking it.
   5. I enjoy watching white mice.

C. The word with the most pleasing connotation is on the left; the least pleasing, on the right. Opinions may vary.

   1. serene/boring
   2. slender/anorexic
   3. famous/notorious
   4. affluent/privileged
   5. educator/lecturer

D. 1. aroma
   2. voluptuous single woman, bargains
   3. strict
   4. dedication (to)
   5. expert, presentation, older gentleman
   6. unusual
   7. competent
   8. distinctive, unemployed
   9. religious beliefs
  10. led

Practicing What You've Learned, p. 173

A. Students will have different responses, but here are some suggestions:

   1. The chemical experiment killed all the fish in the river.
   2. The guest speaker's references to religious cults were inappropriate for a prom banquet.
   3. The fifty-room mausoleum was rotting away and covered with tacky trim and broken ornaments.
   4. Our good-natured father likes to spend time helping us clean the house.
   5. Sandbagging our riverfront property was exhausting, but it brought the neighbors closer together.
   6. My new lawnmower came without a handle and wheels.
   7. Mother Teresa was more dedicated than most of us to helping the poor.

8. The biology textbook lacked a lively voice.
9. I could hear the baby screaming a block away.
10. For only three dollars we got eighteen appetizers, five main courses, and fifteen desserts at the Yugoslavian restaurant.

B. 1. Any new congressional member for our state must comprehend the financial potential of tourism.
2. I thought the $250 rebate on a new set of tires was worth the purchase of a certain brand, but my sister wasn't convinced. I have to go now. Thank you.
3. Farmers may be forced to sell their farms, move to town, and go on welfare.
4. Both Ron Howard and Shirley Temple were successful child actors. As adults they continued their success in different ways: Howard began directing movies and Temple served as a U.S. ambassador to Ghana and Czechoslovakia.
5. Commanders realize they might have to use weapons to destroy another nation's people.
6. Although Jack once thought Jill was sincere, he soon realized she was an unrepentant liar.
7. The City Councilman was furious to learn that his son had been arrested for embezzling funds from the low-income housing project.
8. Never use text abbreviations when writing school assignments or professional correspondence. Talk to you later.
9. The U.S. Embassy in Budapest warned its employees that friendly local women might actually be Hungarian agents.
10. At a press conference on the war in Iraq, former Defense Secretary Donald Rumsfeld announced, "There are things we know and things we don't know."

C. Student responses will vary. Teachers might ask a few students to read their original "blah verb" sentences and their revisions and then ask the class to choose the preferred verbs and sentences.

Discussion of Assignment, p. 174

A. Responses will vary, but a suggestion appears below.

Total preparation time: 35 minutes

Ingredients:

(list is fine)

Directions:

Preheat oven to 375 degrees.

In a large bowl, measure and mix together first six ingredients. In a separate bowl, sift together flour, baking soda, and salt and then carefully blend in the wet ingredients. Fold in chocolate pieces and nuts.

Drop mixture by teaspoonfuls onto ungreased baking sheet about 2 inches apart. Bake 8–10 minutes. Remove and cool. Place cookies in containers and distribute as soon as possible.

This recipe produces six dozen cookies.

B. Again, answers will vary. Teachers might read some of the sentences aloud and allow students to debate which are the most effective. Identify any clichés or Insta-Prose that students do not recognize. This assignment also works well as an in-class small group or whole-class activity.

C. Responses will vary.

Chapter 8
The Reading-Writing Connection, p. 179

■ Summary

How Can Reading Well Help Me Become a Better Writer?

How Can I Become an Analytical Reader?

Steps to Reading Well

- before reading the essay, note publication information and biographical data on the author
- note the title of the essay
- read the essay—noting any key ideas and referring to the dictionary as desired—then briefly summarize your impression of the essay
- review the title and introductory paragraphs again
- locate and mark the thesis
- locate and mark supporting points or ideas
- note how the writer develops, explains, or argues each supporting point
- practice using marginal symbols to mark points of interest
- review the essay's organization
- review the unity and coherence of the essay, noting transitions
- consider the writer's style and the essay's tone

Sample Annotated Essay: "Our Youth Should Serve"—Steven Muller

Practicing What You've Learned

Assignment

Writing a Summary

- read selection carefully and annotate
- when drafting, include the title and author's name in first sentence
- use your own words
- omit references to examples, strategies, and supporting details
- use quotation marks for text that you must borrow
- do not give your own opinion; be objective, accurate, and concise

Practicing What You've Learned

Benefiting from Class Discussions

- try to arrive a few minutes early and review your reading and notes
- remind yourself to become an "active listener"
- turn off pagers, cell phones, and other electronic devices
- listen carefully to your classmates' opinions, offer your own insights, and be willing to voice agreement or polite disagreement
- ask questions or request additional information when necessary for your understanding
- practice thinking critically on two levels: of the essay under review as a draft in which the writer made choices and as an example for ways or reasons to revise your own writing

- take notes and listen for verbal cues to essential material
- develop or borrow a shorthand method for note-taking
- attend every class session and participate actively

Practicing What You've Learned

■ Answers to "Practicing What You've Learned" Exercises

Practicing What You've Learned, p. 185

Student responses will vary.

Practicing What You've Learned, p. 187

Student responses will vary; students may also practice summarizing drafts of their classmates' essays.

Practicing What You've Learned, p. 189

Student responses will vary. This exercise may also provide useful feedback to teachers wishing to know if students thoroughly understood certain material or if they have additional questions.

Part 2
Purposes, Modes, and Strategies

■ **Part Two Summary, p. 193**

Development by Example, Process Analysis, Comparison/Contrast, Definition, Division/Classification, and Causal Analysis

- intends to explain or inform

Argumentation

- intends to convince or persuade

Description

- intends to create a word picture of a person, place, object, or feeling

Narration

- intends to tell a story or recount an event

Writing Essays Using Multiple Strategies

Chapter 9
Exposition, p. 195

■ Summary

The Strategies of Exposition

Strategy One: Development by Example

- examples support, clarify, interest, and persuade
- examples can be brief
- examples can be extended
- examples can explain and clarify
- examples can be used in all types of writing

Developing Your Essay

- select relevant examples
- select strong and convincing examples
- select enough to make each point clear and persuasive

Problems to Avoid

- a lack of specific detail
- a lack of coherence

Essay Topics

A Topic Proposal for Your Essay

- identify subject of your essay and your attitude toward it
- state a reason for your topic choice
- identify your audience(s)
- state your purpose for writing
- list some examples to use for development
- identify potential problems; narrow and refine your focus

Sample Student Essay

Professional Essay

Questions on Content, Structure, and Style

Suggestions for Writing

Vocabulary

A Revision Worksheet

Collaborative Activity

Reviewing Your Progress

Strategy Two: Development by Process Analysis

Directional versus Informative

Developing Your Essay

- select an appropriate subject
- describe any necessary equipment
- define special terms
- state steps in a logical, chronological order
- explain each step clearly, sufficiently, accurately
- organize steps effectively

Problems to Avoid

- don't forget to include a thesis
- pay special attention to the conclusion

Essay Topics

A Topic Proposal for Your Essay

- identify your subject as either directional or informative
- determine your subject's complexity
- state a reason for your topic choice
- identify your audience(s)
- identify your purpose
- list at least three steps or stages in the process
- identify potential problems

Sample Student Essay

Professional Essays

- The Informative Process Essay

Questions on Content, Structure, and Style

Suggestions for Writing

Vocabulary

- The Directional Process Essay

Questions on Content, Structure, and Style

Suggestions for Writing

Vocabulary

A Revision Worksheet

Collaborative Activity

Reviewing Your Progress

Strategy Three: Development by Comparison and Contrast

Developing Your Essay

- point-by-point pattern
- block pattern

43

Which Pattern Should You Use?

- audition both patterns in the prewriting stage

Problems to Avoid

- the "so what?" thesis is the most serious error
- describe your subjects clearly and distinctly
- avoid a choppy essay

Essay Topics

A Topic Proposal for Your Essay

- identify the two subjects and some ways in which they are similar/different
- determine whether to compare or contrast
- determine your purpose
- identify your audience(s)
- list three or four points of comparison or contrast
- identify potential problems, including the "so what?" factor

Sample Student Essays

- The Point-by-Point Pattern
- The Block Pattern

Professional Essays

- The Point-by-Point Pattern

Questions on Content, Structure, and Style

Suggestions for Writing

Vocabulary

- The Block Pattern

Questions on Content, Structure, and Style

Suggestions for Writing

Vocabulary

A Revision Worksheet

Collaborative Activity

A Special Kind of Comparison: The Analogy

A comparison that uses one thing to clarify or argue a second thing

- use to clarify and explain
- use to argue and persuade or to help support an idea
- use to dramatize or capture an image

Problems to Avoid

- don't use trite, unclear, or illogical analogies
- don't substitute an analogy for other kinds of evidence to support points of an argument
- don't use analogies as "scare tactics"

Reviewing Your Progress

- determine which part of your essay you like the best and why
- determine which point of comparison or contrast you think is most successful and why
- determine which part of the essay gave you the most trouble and how you overcame the problem
- determine which part of the essay you would revisit if time permitted
- determine what you learned about the topic and what you learned about yourself as a writer

44

Strategy Four: Development by Definition

Dictionary versus Humorous versus Extended

Why Do We Define?

We define
- to clarify the abstract
- to provide personal interpretation of the vague, controversial, or misunderstood
- to explain the new or unusual (slang, dialect, or jargon)
- to make understandable the unfamiliar
- to offer information to a particular audience
- to inform or entertain by presenting a word's interesting history, uses, or effects

Developing Your Essay

- know your purpose
- give your readers a reason to read
- keep your audience in mind to anticipate and avoid problems of clarity
- use as many strategies as necessary to clarify your definition
  1. describe parts or categories
  2. state examples
  3. compare/contrast similarities
  4. explain a process
  5. provide familiar synonyms
  6. define by negation
  7. trace history/development or changes from original linguistic meaning
  8. discuss causes or effects
  9. identify times/places of use
  10. associate with recognizable people, places, or ideas

Problems to Avoid

Don't:
- present an incomplete definition
- introduce your essay with a quotation from *Webster's*
- define vaguely or by using generalities
- offer circular definitions

Essay Topics

A Topic Proposal for Your Essay

- identify your subject and determine whether to define it subjectively or objectively
- state a reason for your topic choice
- identify your audience(s)
- determine your purpose
- list at least two techniques to help you define terms
- identify potential problems

Sample Student Essay

Professional Essay

Questions on Content, Structure, and Style

Suggestions for Writing

Vocabulary

A Revision Worksheet

Collaborative Activity

Reviewing Your Progress

Strategy Five: Development by Division and Classification

- Division is the act of separating something into its component parts.
- Classification is the systematic grouping of a number of things into categories.

Developing Your Essay

- select one principle of classification or division and stick to it
- state the purpose of your division or classification
- account for all the parts in your division or classification

Problems to Avoid

- underdeveloped categories
- indistinct categories
- too few or too many categories

Essay Topics

A Topic Proposal for Your Essay

- identify your subject and determine whether to classify or divide
- determine which principle of classification or division to use
- state a reason for your topic choice
- identify your audience(s)
- list at least three categories for development
- identify potential problems

Sample Student Essay

Professional Essay: Classification

Questions on Content, Structure, and Style

Suggestions for Writing

Vocabulary

Professional Essay: Division

Questions on Content, Structure, and Style

Suggestions for Writing

Vocabulary

A Revision Worksheet

Collaborative Activity

Reviewing Your Progress

Strategy Six: Development by Causal Analysis

Cause is the condition that produces something; it asks, "Why does/did/will X happen?"
Effect is the result produced by something; it asks, "What does/did/will Y produce?"

Developing Your Essay

- present a reasonable thesis statement
- limit your essay to a discussion of recent, major causes or effects
- organize your essay clearly
- convince your reader that a causal relationship exists by showing how the relationship works

Problems to Avoid

- don't oversimplify
- avoid the *post hoc* fallacy
- avoid circular logic

Essay Topics

A Topic Proposal for Your Essay

- identify your subject and purpose; narrow subject and focus
- determine your method of development
- state a reason for your topic choice
- identify your audience(s)
- list at least two major causes or effects
- identify potential problems

Sample Student Essay

Professional Essay

Questions on Content, Structure, and Style

Suggestions for Writing

Vocabulary

A Revision Worksheet

Collaborative Activity

Reviewing Your Progress

■ Discussion, Answers to Questions, Vocabulary

1. Example

"So What's So Bad About Being So-So?" by Lisa Wilson Strick—p. 205

Discussion

Strick's essay, originally published in 1984, appeared at a time of heightened awareness of the competitiveness of American society. Do college students today still perceive overzealous competition as a problem in the United States? A lively discussion could result by asking students to agree or disagree with Strick's contention that "in today's competitive world we have to be 'experts.' " Ask them to support their views with specific examples in the same manner that Strick supports her thesis.

Answers to Questions, p. 207

1. It is an example that introduces the thesis.
2. The thesis is implied throughout the essay, but is stated clearly and without equivocation in the next-to-last paragraph: "I think it's time we put a stop to all this . . . and . . . enjoy being a beginner again." Our many leisure-time activities were meant to be enjoyed, not necessarily mastered.
3. The major examples are from hobbies; perhaps more could have been offered from school. The first, running, refers to the pervasive concern for and availability of equipment. In this case, it is the right shoes, another area of specialization that wasn't a concern in the old days when anything to protect your feet would do. The dancing example continues the emphasis on the proper costume and hours of intense classes. The next three, knitting, soccer, and gymnastics, also illustrate her point.
4. Too much competition drains the fun out of an experience. Her piano playing irritates her son, running without the proper equipment is an embarrassment to serious athletes, "real" dancers don't just mess around with a few steps, and "if children can't attain a high level of expertise in soccer, gymnastics, and foreign languages, it is as if their time and effort were wasted. Children don't seem to be able to have fun anymore, as reflected by the daughter in paragraph 8 who muses, "Well, I don't actually have a lot of free time."
5. In paragraph 4, informal verbs like "pulling on" your sneakers and "slogging" are in contrast to formal ones like "plan" and "log." In addition, the mention of "leather or canvas," the type of sole, and the brand of shoe are nice contrasts to her image of an earlier time when a concern for such fine points was unnecessary. Paragraph 6 has a long sentence full of details about the reindeer sweater. The form of the sentence reinforces the point Strick is making about how general knowledge is not sufficient; these days you have to add all sorts of little touches that demonstrate your great skill. A sentence in paragraph 8 is similar, only this time the subject is early childhood education; in addition to soccer lessons at age three, Strick throws in parenthetical references to preschool diving, creative writing, and Suzuki clarinet. Most of the other paragraphs have a similar depth and breadth of detail.
6. Dialogue makes the points of the essay more real and personal. If readers feel the author is overly picky, quotations from real people tend to soften this impression.
7. The solution is to take up an activity without ever intending to become good at it. Strick uses the example of two-year-olds to give adults an idea of how to change their attitude and get on the road to a happier lifestyle. Presumably, two-year-olds have not yet been infected with that competitive spirit.
8. Although there are many occasions when Strick is humorous, overall the tone of the essay is that of a person who is genuinely concerned about the way we live our lives and wants us to change our habits. She uses phrases like "Have you noticed?" or "We used to do these things for fun," and she even acknowledges that what she is criticizing has some merit ("Ambition, drive and the desire to excel are all admirable within limits"), all of which gives her suggestions and point of view credibility. Since this is not a scholarly treatise intended for presentation at a conference of sociology professors, the breezy informality of the piece will be more interesting to a general reader. Also, since many of these readers are deeply affected by the lifestyle Strick describes, her gently humorous but pointed comments are more likely to be taken seriously; Strick seems to be the neighbor we all have or are, and we share her concerns as well as her frustration.
9. The conclusion wraps up the essay by putting into practice (not too much, of course!) the process Strick has just suggested: take up an activity with no intention of becoming good at it.
10. Student agreement/disagreement should be well supported with specific examples.

Vocabulary

1. errant (2)—roving, straying, wandering
2. incompetence (3)—lack of necessary ability
3. aficionados (4)—enthusiastic admirers or followers
4. mediocrity (4)—average to below-average ability
5. excel (9)—to surpass or do better than others
6. fluent (9)—flowing smoothly or gracefully; most often used to describe those who speak and write foreign languages well
7. zest (11)—spirited enjoyment; gusto

2. Process Analysis: Informative

"To Bid the World Farewell" by Jessica Mitford—p. 218

Discussion

Mitford's essay shows students that process papers can have a purpose beyond the simple spreading of "how-to-do-it" information. Students frequently become involved in a debate over Mitford's belief that this "prettying up" of the dead is excessive and absurd, with some arguing that the elaborate funeral ritual is essential for the living and others attacking it as sham. Such a debate might lead some students to investigate the legal burial requirements in their state and then to write an essay about their findings. And while many students find this essay distasteful, most agree that Mitford has performed a valuable service by publicizing the process so that people have enough information to make a choice regarding their own funeral or that of relatives. This essay provides an excellent opportunity to discuss use of vivid, sensory details and their effects on the reader. Mitford's carefully selected word choice ("the embalmer . . . returns to the attack") should be analyzed as the class discusses the essay's tone. This essay may also be used to introduce such terms as euphemism and personification; Mitford's easily recognized transition devices might emphasize a lesson on coherence.

Answers to Questions, p. 222

1. Mitford feels that, in contrast to earlier days, Americans are now paying millions for a process they know nothing about. The reason is not the gruesomeness of the subject nor Americans' lack of curiosity, but the almost universal desire of undertakers to keep the process a secret. Mitford implies that if people did understand the embalming process, they might begin to question whether they wanted or needed such a service. Her attitude toward the morticians is critical; she obviously believes that people should have access to information on the embalming process.

2. Yes. There are numerous examples of descriptions that appeal to the senses. Below are listed only a few:

    Sight: "Positioning the lips is a problem. The lips should give the impression of being ever so slightly parted. . . . Up drift can sometimes be remedied by pushing one or two straight pins through the inner margin of the lower lip and then inserting them between the two front upper teeth" (paragraph 9).

    Smell: "About three to six gallons of a dyed and perfumed solution of formaldehyde, glycerin, borax, phenol, alcohol and water is soon circulating through Mr. Jones . . ." (paragraph 9).

    Touch: "If Flextone is used . . . the skin retains a velvety softness, the tissues are rubbery and pliable" (paragraph 8).

3. Mitford wants her readers to identify and sympathize with the corpse, to understand that the body suffering such indignities was once a living person.

4. Mitford feels that this process is unnecessary, expensive, and degrading. Her tone may be described as ironic or sarcastic. To "have at" him makes Mr. Jones seem like a piece of meat, as does "returning to the attack" in the next example. The other comments are ironic because Mr. Jones _is_ dead (not "well"), _is_ in a box for burial, and cannot possibility host a social event.

5. She quotes the undertakers and textbooks to show the funeral business's crass and depersonalized treatment of the dead. They seem preoccupied with the need to artificially "beautify" the body, regardless of the means (kitchen cleanser and nail polish on the teeth, pins in the lips, wire through the jaw, etc.). The dead person becomes little more than a department store dummy to be dressed for some sort of freak fashion show. Mitford quotes the undertakers themselves to show the readers that the callous descriptions are not her words but theirs. The quote in paragraph 7 says that even though research on embalming is "haphazard," undertakers are advised (for "best results") to begin embalming before life is "completely extinct," that is, before all the body's cells are dead. Mitford implies that undertakers might be so eager to achieve those best results that they might begin too soon; but she ironically concludes that at least there is no risk of accidentally burying anyone alive: after all, embalming removes the blood.

6. Mitford quotes euphemisms such as "Repose Block" and "Slumber Room" to show how the funeral business tries to sugarcoat death for the living by pretending the dead person is only asleep or resting. Terms such as "dermasurgeon" are used to give embalmers more prestige by linking their work to that of physicians, especially plastic surgeons.

7. The words in paragraph 10 connote a defenseless person being attacked by the mortician. The series of questions in paragraph 12 reproduces the flippant tone Mitford thinks characterizes the embalmer's attitude toward the bodies. The corpse is not a dead person worthy of respect but merely a challenge to the embalmer's ingenuity. One can almost hear Mitford's sarcastic imitation of a mortician saying, "Head off ? Hey, no problem."

8. Yes. Beginning with paragraph 4: "first" (paragraphs 3–4); "preparation room" (4–5); "first," "embalming" (5–6); "another" (6–7); "to return to" (7–8); "soon," "Mr. Jones" (8–9); "The next step" (9–10); "all this attention" (10–11); "returns" (11–12); "The opposite condition" (12–13); parallel construction of "If Mr. Jones . . ." (14–15); "completed," "now" (15–16); "now ready" (16–17); "next" (17–18).

9. Yes. The idea of a corpse holding "open house" for visitors is ridiculous. But ridiculous, according to Mitford, is the correct term for what embalmers try to do: dress up and beautify a dead body as if it were hosting a party.

10. Some students may argue that the funeral business makes it easier for the living to accept the death of a friend or relative and that this comfort justifies the artificial "dandifying" of the body. Others may agree with Mitford, adding that the cost of funerals today is also unreasonable.

Vocabulary

1. docility (1)—meekness, obedience
2. perpetuation (1)—continuance
3. inherent (2)—basic, intrinsic
4. mandatory (2)—obligatory
5. intractable (3)—obstinate, not easily governed or controlled
6. reticence (3)—reluctance
7. raison d'être (3)—French for "reason to be"
8. ingenious (5)—brilliant
9. cadaver (5)—a dead body
10. somatic (7)—pertaining to, or affecting, the body
11. rudimentary (7)—basic, elementary
12. dispel (7)—remove

13. pliable (8)—easily bent, supple
14. semblance (11)—form or outward appearance
15. ravages (11)—violently destructive effects
16. stippling (12)—painting by means of dots or small spots
17. emaciation (13)—wasted or depleted condition

2A. Process Analysis: Directional

"Preparing for the Job Interview: Know Thyself" by Katy Piotrowski—p. 224

Discussion

Piotrowski's essay is a brief but thorough step-by-step analysis of how to prepare for a job interview.

Answers to Questions, p. 225

1. The process described prepares job candidates by giving them the steps to follow to prepare and present themselves for an interview.
2. The author gives step-by-step directions on how to proceed from preparation through the end of the interview.
3. The following are the steps involved in preparing for the interview:
    a) identify three responsibilities of the job;
    b) describe at least three examples from your past that demonstrate expertise in those areas and think of other experiences in your professional life that might show you as a viable candidate—describe the situation or tasks, talk about the actions you took, finish with the results of your efforts, and frame your answers using action verbs that show leadership;
    c) prepare and practice general information about your work history highlights, education, and why you are excited about the job;
    d) investigate the company to which you are applying—its goals, products, services, and recent publicity;
    e) think about questions you can ask the employer; and
    f) thank the interviewer(s) for their time.
4. The organizational structure follows the steps in the order they should be taken. By using Shawn—a real person—to explain the process, Piotrowski is able to illustrate the steps with specific examples and details, which clarifies her advice.
5. Piotrowski's examples further our understanding of what she means by certain terms. They also provide choices, as in paragraph 6, of ideas that might otherwise be difficult to narrow down.
6. "First" (2), "moving on" (3), "in addition to" (4), "As well as" (5) are some paragraph openers that help transition. The author also uses content, for example, staying on the topic of questions at the end of paragraph 5 and beginning of paragraph 6.
7. She advises against negotiating salary and warns against forgetting to thank the interviewers, but in a larger way she is warning candidates to be prepared.
8. In paragraph 3, Piotrowski numbers the steps of the subprocess and gives it the acronym, STAR, to distinguish it from the larger process.
9. Her tone is friendly and professional. It is appropriate and effective; she allows us to participate in a professional experience and eases the tension for us. She begins with her narrative, which invites us into the conversation. Shawn is gently "prompted," "reminded," and praised ("impressive responses").
10. The conclusion helps to frame the essay by returning our attention to Shawn and revealing that she got the job, thus showing the reader that the methods he or she just learned actually work.

51

Vocabulary

1. expertise (2)—extensive knowledge and experience
2. implemented (3)—conducted or installed, coordinated
3. prospective (5)—potential, viable

3. Comparison and Contrast: Point-by-Point Pattern

"Grant and Lee: A Study in Contrasts" by Bruce Catton—p. 239

Discussion

This is one of the most famous (and most frequently anthologized) essays that students will come across. The author is well known for his encyclopedic knowledge of and writings about the Civil War, and this excerpt reflects not only that knowledge but also Catton's empathy for the period and many of the principal characters of that tragic conflict. It is also a concrete example of the three ways to avoid what Wyrick calls the "so what?" thesis. The subject has a universal appeal—it demonstrates something about principled soldiers in a native American conflict that can apply to us all, even if we are not in a "war," but merely in an argument. It is directed to Americans interested in a vital part of our history, and it especially shows "a particular relationship between two subjects." The major method of organization—contrast—announces itself in the title, and the development is essentially by the "point-by-point" method. There is, however, some comparison at the end that provides not only some perspective, but an effective conclusion as well.

Answers to Questions, p. 242

1. The thesis is contained in all of paragraph 3.
2. A good summary of Lee's view of society is in paragraph 5, where Catton states that Lee represented "the age of chivalry transplanted to a New World." The old idea of the Great Chain of Being is a good analogy to Lee's social ideal. Some were higher on the chain than others, but those higher up needed to see their favored position not as a justification for abusing those lower down, but as a position of responsibility from which they had the means and the power to improve society as a whole and not just their own lot in life. Catton describes Lee in terms that might also be applied to, say, the men of the Kennedy dynasty: the quintessential man of leisure whose concern for his version of society makes him not only a great defender of a humanitarian aristocracy, but an even greater symbol of what the South stood for and what Confederate soldiers were fighting for.
3. Catton describes Grant as both the product and the embodiment of the pioneers and the pioneer spirit. These people looked at the social structure of the country as virtually nonexistent, except as it promoted and defended the principle that society serves the individual, not the other way around. It was the rugged individuals who tamed the land west of the mountains, fought uncountable odds to survive, and forged a democracy from their labors. "As [the Nation's] horizons expanded, so did [the individual's]," and everyone could be anything they wished, uninhibited by class or other social restrictions. It was the raucous vitality of those stimulated by the newness of the land and the society, not the reasoned judgments of those representing the old social class of the landed gentry, that gave America its spirit and energy.
4. Catton uses the point-by-point pattern to develop his essay in paragraphs 4–16, contrasting the generals' backgrounds, philosophies, and the views they embodied as well as comparing their shared personal traits.
5. Catton begins to compare the greatness in each man—the fact that they were both great fighters, had enormous tenacity, were daring and resourceful, and could turn quickly from war to peace.

52

6. Within paragraphs, Catton tends to move from general to specific, to set up a background or milieu, and then place one general and then the other within it as an outgrowth of his particular background or social circumstance. For example, "Lee was tidewater Virginia. . . . A land that was beginning all over again . . . In such a land . . . was . . . [a] class of men who lived not to gain advantage for themselves . . . [and] Lee embodied the noblest elements of this aristocratic ideal." Catton not only varies the sentence structure and length to avoid choppiness, he even uses sentence structure to emphasize a point, like the short "individual" sentences in paragraph 8 that are not woven together as tightly as in other paragraphs and thereby "compete" on their own for attention, much like people did on the frontier. Between paragraphs, Catton uses transition words like "yet" and "lastly" as well as repeating words and phrases from previous material. Paragraph 7, for example, begins "Grant . . . was everything Lee was not."

7. As befits his status as one of our best writers, Catton states his intentions in topic sentences and then delivers what he promises. In paragraph 8, for example, the topic is how the frontier men were opposites of the tidewater aristocrats. Each sentence in the paragraph is unified coherently around the topic, and each has its own minicontrast around that point. In paragraph 5, each sentence is devoted to describing in ever more detail the tidewater Virginia background of Lee. Catton could perhaps be faulted for not including enough concrete detail, going no further than abstractions like "solemn obligations" or "self-reliant to a fault," but overall, there seems to be enough detail to make the points of contrast between the two men.

8. The advantage of the single sentence in paragraph 3 is that it isolates the thesis and provides a break from the introductory material in paragraph 2. Paragraph 4 is like a headline announcing the beginning of the contrast as well as the key element of the description of both men—an old aristocracy in a new world. In Lee's case, Catton shows how Lee embodied this aristocracy; in Grant's case, Catton highlights how different Grant was from that old aristocratic notion.

9. Catton has a high opinion of both, and the tone is admiring but not fawning. This tone creates an atmosphere that is neither frivolous nor hostile to one side, reflecting, again, Catton's balanced admiration for both of these great Americans. The aristocratic South, always easy to criticize as not conducive to democratic ideals and structures, is portrayed by Catton as populated by people meeting "solemn obligations" and looking to its leadership "to give it strength and virtue." Similarly, the individual pioneer was not merely a competitive animal, but one who had a "deep sense of belonging to a national community." The tone of the essay, therefore, comes across as neither argumentative nor merely informative, nor aggressively jingoistic but appropriately serious, thoughtful, and (most important) empathetic to both men who have come to represent two significant regions of the United States.

10. The comparison of both men turning quickly from war to peace suggests the end of the war, the end of their roles as generals, and their final meeting as a paradigm of what the relationship between the North and the South should now be. The end of the essay suggests the scene at the beginning, and as this moment in history ends, so does the essay.

Vocabulary

1. chivalry (5)—social behavior reflecting that idealized by medieval knights, i.e., politeness, honor, self-sacrifice
2. deportment (5)—body language, behavior
3. embodied (6)—an abstraction made concrete
4. tenacity (11)—the quality of holding on for a long time
5. diametrically (12)—totally opposite
6. burgeoning (12)—growing, ballooning
7. indomitable (14)—unbeatable, unable to be dominated
8. reconciliation (16)—the settlement or resolution of a dispute

3A. Comparison and Contrast: Block Method

"Two Ways of Viewing the River" by Samuel Clemens—p. 243

Discussion

While many students will have read the novels of Samuel Clemens (Mark Twain), few of them may be familiar with his essays. "Two Ways of Viewing the River" is an intriguing piece for class discussion since rather than contrasting two different subjects, as is most often done (see "Grant and Lee: A Study in Contrasts"), Clemens presents two vastly different perspectives of the same subject. It might be emphasized that the actual features of the river remain the same (the sunset, the floating log); it is Clemens's vision of the river that has changed. Students might be asked to complete a timed, in-class freewriting exercise in which they contrast two very different perspectives they have had of one unchanging subject. For example, they might contrast their first impression with a later view of someone they now know well. Discussion of these student writings could reveal the importance of descriptive detail in comparison/contrast essays.

Answers to Questions, p. 244

1. Clemens is contrasting his personal, emotional view of the river when he was new to steamboating with his later view as a captain. His thesis is embodied in the first three sentences: While a captain's perspective is valuable and gives a sense of accomplishment, it has sadly replaced an earlier, mystical connection to the river.

2. Clemens chooses the block method of development. One reason this choice is appropriate is because he can contrast the same observations (e.g., the floating log, the tall dead tree) in each block; a reader would not get lost in the points of contrast from block to block. A more significant reason that this is not only an appropriate choice, but also may be the best choice for this selection is that the first block sets a mood in its totality that is necessary to understand before the reader can understand the loss implied in the more sterile and cold second block.

3. The second sentence in paragraph 2 provides a transition for the reader. Clemens moves the reader ahead in time to a later view of the river "when I began to cease from noting the glories and the charms which the moon and the sun and the twilight wrought upon the river's face."

4. Clemens's reference to doctors in the final paragraph presents a parallel experience to his own and reemphasizes his thesis.

5. The questions encourage the reader to think about a more universal application of Clemens's experience. The last question asks the reader to think further: Is the loss of innocent wonder and splendor worth the gain of accomplishment and professionalism?

6. The language in paragraph 1 is rich, lush, sensual, and poetic. The diction appropriately creates the mood of wonder and magnificence for the reader to contrast to the more businesslike language of the second view.

7. These similes provide concrete visual images of beauty for the reader: "as many-tinted as an opal…"; "trail that shone . . . like silver."

8. The language in paragraph 2 is sparse and practical. The visions and feelings relative to the river are unimportant; only the usefulness of the objects and the dangers created by them are important to a good captain.

9. Clemens personifies the "new snag" when he claims it will "fish for steamboats." This personification adds a certain element of alienation and antagonism to his later view of the river, which contrasts sharply with his earlier perspective.

10. The mood of each contrasting block is distinctly different—the earlier block is warm and sensual while the latter is professional. Throughout the selection, Clemens presents a sense of nostalgia and loss.

Vocabulary

1. trifling (1)—being of small value or importance
2. acquisition (1)—something gained
3. conspicuous (1)—easy to see; attracting attention
4. ruddy (1)—reddish; glowing
5. wrought (2)—fashioned or made, usually with great care
6. compassing (3)—providing direction for

4. Definition

"The Munchausen Mystery" by Don R. Lipsitt—p. 257

Discussion

Discussing the clarity with which Lipsitt defines this complex syndrome for a lay reader provides the opportunity to discuss the importance of audience considerations in a definition essay. What words and techniques indicate the targeted audience? Students might research a professional definition of this disease (or *hypochondria*) and compare the two. What are the different purposes? While the reason writers define terms and concepts for lay audiences is rather obvious, professional definitions are necessary for other reasons. Why would a writer define a term for his or her peers? After discussing terms and concepts on which students are the experts, they might practice writing two definitions of one of these terms, one for someone at a similar level as themselves and one for a novice reader.

Answers to Questions, p. 259

1. The example illustrates the syndrome that Lipsitt will define. A reader will immediately see the intriguing—mystifying—nature of this strange condition.
2. The title indicates a strangeness and puzzling quality to this disease, which makes for much more reader interest than a title that would merely suggest a practical definition.
3. Because of the large number of Munchausen patients, the condition accounts for enormous expenses for the health-care system, expenses that are usually not reimbursed.
4. Knowing the origin of the name increases the reader's understanding of the fictional nature of the condition and the wandering of the patient from one medical provider to the next. Also, the unusual name might leave a lingering question in the reader's mind if it were not addressed.
5. Without the specific examples, a reader could hardly imagine the extremes to which a patient goes to feign illness.
6. The specific patients illustrate the extent to which these individuals persist in their charades. Students might believe an extended example of one particular patient might be even more interesting and instructive.
7. By contrasting Munchausen to hypochondria, Lipsitt refines the definition more distinctly. Munchausen involves not only false illness, but intentional, conscious deception.
8. When Lipsitt explains the causes of Munchausen, he anticipates a typical reader's question, as most would wonder why anyone would try so compulsively to deceive physicians. Also, a full (extended) definition of any disease should include its causes in order to understand its progression.
9. The conclusion is effective because it acknowledges what little is known (and has been explained in the definition) about the syndrome while suggesting there is yet more to learn before its occurrence can be reduced.
10. Student responses will vary.

1. fabricates (1)—makes up
2. mimic (2)—imitate
3. incurs (2)—meets with
4. hypochondriacs (4)—persons who believe they are ill
5. sputum (4)—saliva, spit
6. palpably (4)—obviously, easily perceived
7. feasible (4)—reasonable, workable
8. psychoanalytic (7)—pertaining to a method of treating mental disorders by analysis
9. paradoxically (7)—in a seemingly impossible manner
10. odyssey (9)—a long and complicated journey

5. Division and Classification: Classification

"The Plot against People" by Russell Baker—p. 268

Discussion

As Baker's essay is comic in tone and his purpose is to entertain, class discussion of humor writing is valid here, particularly as many freshman composition students will want to try their hand at comic writing at some point in the course. Ask students if the 1968 publication date limits the effectiveness of Baker's essay in present day. Is it dated in any way? If so, what parts of the essay are dated, and which still seem fresh and effective? Note the importance of word choice. For example, Baker consistently refers to "man" and "mankind." Would this language be considered sexist today? If they were to update Baker's essay, what changes would student writers make? Why?

Answers to Questions, p. 269

1. Baker's purpose is to entertain his audience by presenting humorous truisms they are likely to empathize with and understand.
2. The thesis statement is the opening sentence of his essay. While students might argue that a more fully developed lead-in would be effective, it should be noted that Baker's direct statement of focus has an appeal of its own as it cuts directly to the essay's subject and provokes the thoughts of the reader.
3. Baker's categories for inanimate objects include "those that don't work, those that break down and those that get lost." He classifies these objects according to behavior—"The method each object uses to achieve its purpose," which is to "resist" and "ultimately defeat" humankind.
4. Baker gives examples to illustrate each category fully and to allow his audience to empathize; readers will recognize the purse that disappears, the furnace that breaks down, and the flashlight that never works. The specifics are a strength of Baker's essay.
5. The category "those that break down" is particularly well developed. Students might cite the example of the automobile (paragraphs 2, 3, and 4). Or, if students argue that "those that get lost" is particularly vivid, the example of the lost purse might be mentioned (paragraphs 8 and 10).
6. Some examples of personification in the essay include the automobile "with the cunning typical of its breed," the notion that appliances are "in league" to cause maximum frustration for humans, and the idea that "those that don't work" "have truly defeated man by conditioning him never to expect anything of them." This personification is a key part of Baker's humor.
7. Baker's mock-scientific word choice is important to the essay's success (e.g., "Some persons believe this constitutes evidence that inanimate objects are not entirely hostile to man"). A serious essay on

this subject is likely to fail because of lack of purpose. Would anyone actually enjoy a factual essay that notes that purses do, indeed, get lost, and automobiles do, in fact, break down?

8. The essay's title reveals the common link between the categories as Baker establishes his "us versus them" comic tone.

9. One way to change Baker's language for gender concerns is to use plural nouns and pronouns in lieu of references to "man" and any male pronouns. For example in paragraph two, instead of "man" we can use "people" and instead of "him" we can use "us." In paragraph 7 we can delete "no man" and use "no one," whereas deleting "to man" in paragraph 11 still maintains the sense of the sentence, and replacing "a man" with "some" will also suffice. In paragraph 16, "us" and "we" will work, whereas we need to use a possessive in 17, such as "our."

10. Instructors might note that Baker's essay appeared in a newspaper, whose style demands short paragraphs. Students might practice writing conclusions by creating a new, less-abrupt, ending for this essay.

Vocabulary

1. inanimate (1)—lifeless, inorganic
2. cunning (3)—craftiness, slyness
3. evolve (6)—develop, unfold, produce
4. locomotion (7)—movement
5. virtually (9)—practically
6. inherent (10)—essential, innate
7. constitutes (11)—forms, establishes, sets up
8. conciliatory (12)—appeasing, forgiving
9. barometer (13)—instrument that measures atmospheric pressure and helps weather prediction

5A. Division and Classifications: Division

"What is REALLY in a Hot Dog?" by the staff of SixWise—p. 270

Discussion

Despite rumors about pig snouts and chicken beaks, almost everyone in America has eaten a hot dog at some point in life. This article illustrates the strategy of division as it explains the parts—the ingredients—that can make up this popular food. Students should see how division may be used to support a point of view as well as offering information. This article may also offer teachers an opportunity to discuss the persuasiveness and reliability of Web sites and online articles.

Answers to Questions, p. 272

1. Classification groups things into categories; division separates something into its parts or components (hot dog into its ingredients).

2. This article presents unpleasant descriptions of hot dog ingredients and the health risks that are associated with hot dog consumption. Health conscious readers may be most interested in this article.

3. The figures on hot dog consumption and sales illustrate the hot dog's popularity.

4. The statement from the National Hot Dog and Sausage Council presents a benign description of the hot dog's ingredients. This description allows the authors to then give readers "the real story"—that is, a description of possible ingredients (disgusting and/or risky) that the Council avoided mentioning.

5. Direct quotes from the U.S. Department of Agriculture and the U.S. Food Safety and Inspection Service lend credibility to the article.

57

6. Readers are warned about the various meats and meat byproducts that hot dogs may contain. Student responses will vary.
7. This paragraph could be strengthened by adding supporting quotes from credible sources that link the consumption of processed meats with cancer.
8. Dr. Blaylock's testimony is meant to give credibility to the argument that hot dog consumption may cause serious health related problems.
9. This article is subjective. The writers advocate eating healthier varieties of hot dogs, such as organic, nitrate-free varieties that contain all meat and no byproducts or other artificial additives.
10. Student responses will vary.

Vocabulary

1. delve (1)—to carry on intensive and thorough research
2. snouts (1)—the part of an animal's head projecting forward and containing the nose and jaws
3. damper (2)—a person or thing that depresses
4. caveats (3)—a warning or caution
5. sieve (3)—an instrument with a mesh or perforated bottom, used for separating course from fine parts of loose matter
6. carcass (4)—the dead body of an animal

6. Causal Analysis

"Some Lessons from the Assembly Line" by Andrew Braaksma—p. 282

Discussion

Braaksma's essay is a lesson in the realities of blue-collar work. He claims that working on an assembly line in a factory during the summer months away from school, rather than taking on easier part-time work, has given him a clearer perspective of what his life would have been like if he hadn't gone to college and then what his college education really means to his future.

Answers to Questions, p. 284

1. Braaksma appreciates school because he works summers in a factory and finds the work harder than schoolwork. The essay focuses on the lessons he has learned (the effects of the job).
2. He has learned how lucky he is to get an education, how to work hard, and how easy it is to lose work, and he is inspired to make the most of college before entering the "real" world.
3. He begins with a brief narrative that then compares and contrasts his school environment to his work environment. He continues to contrast his expectations to his reality, his job to other students' jobs and his perspective to theirs, his long hours to his pay check, his own future reality to that of his coworkers, his luck to those without it, his laziness at school to his hard work at the factory, and his time on the line to that of his coworkers.
4. "Stamping, cutting, welding, moving, assembling" are some of the verbs that reveal his work. He also mentions work beginning at 6:00 a. m., an environment of "hulking, spark-showering machines," and "schedules and quotas" that are "rigid."
5. Paragraph 1 details the sights and sounds of the factory, whereas 2 describes his work. Paragraph 4 compares hours to pay and details problems with machinery and employers. Paragraph 5 reveals his expectation to go to college and his reality there of skipping classes and turning in lazy work, while paragraph 6 reveals reactions of coworkers to his textbooks.

6. He does this to show the meaning of real work—that it is hard and can't be abused in the way schoolwork can. Some readers will be offended, but most will probably nod in agreement. He values the hard work he has learned to perform, despite his desire to avoid it in the future.

7. His sense of guilt comes from knowing that he is taking a job from someone who may need it and doesn't have the means to go to college. Moreover, he has the opportunity to escape the oppression of factory work every fall and spring, while others will toil away their whole lives.

8. The dialogue here helps to make his coworkers real to the reader. It also adds a perspective that helps support Braaksma's sense of guilt and his understanding that it isn't just he who finds the work hard.

9. He begins with the French literature class that he tone is a long way from factory life, so that when he returns to the class in the end he is referencing the quality of life he leads as a student and appreciating his new understanding that he came to learn the hard way.

10. Responses will vary.

Vocabulary

1. blue-collar (2)—reference to workers who toil with their hands in factories, as opposed to white-collar work that relates to those who wear white shirts in offices
2. lush (2)—full of botanical greenery
3. cavernous (2)—large, deep, and dark as a cave
4. cocksure (4)—arrogant
5. downsizing (4)—a term used by big business to indicate layoffs and cutbacks
6. tinged (6)—tainted, hued, or suggesting a color, feeling, or idea
7. voyeuristic (6)—having a sense of watching others without them knowing
8. discreetly (6)—quietly or politely, tactfully or judiciously

Chapter 10
Argumentation, p. 287

■ **Summary**

Developing Your Essay

- choose an appropriate title
- explore possibilities and your opinions
- anticipate opposing views
- know and remember your audience
- decide which points of argument to include
- organize clearly (patterns A, B, C, and combination)
- argue logically (by example, comparison/contrast, cause/effect, definition)
- offer evidence to support claims (personal experience, testimony, facts, statistics, etc.)
- find appropriate tone
- consider Rogerian techniques if appropriate

Problems to Avoid

Common Logical Fallacies

- hasty generalizations
- *non sequitur*
- begging the question
- red herring
- *post hoc, ergo propter hoc*
- *ad hominem*
- faulty use of authority
- *ad populum*
- circular thinking
- either/or
- hypostatization
- bandwagon appeal
- straw man
- faulty analogy
- quick fix

Practicing What You've Learned

Assignment

Collaborative Activity

Essay Topics

A Topic Proposal for Your Essay

- identify the subject of your argument and write a rough opinion statement
- state at least one reason for choosing this topic

- identify your audience and purpose
- list at least two reasons that support your opinion
- clearly state at least one opposing opinion
- identify any difficulties that might arise during drafting

Sample Student Essay

Professional Essays

Questions on Content, Structure, and Style

Suggestions for Writing

Vocabulary

Analyzing Advertisements

- Conflicting Positions: Gun Control
- Competing Products: Sources of Energy
- Popular Appeals: Spending Our Money

Practicing What You've Learned

A Revision Worksheet

Collaborative Activity

Reviewing Your Progress

■ Answers to "Practicing What You've Learned" Exercises

Practicing What You've Learned, p. 299

A. Numbers 1, 6, 7, 9, 10, and 13 argue for allowing homeschoolers to play. Numbers 2, 3, 4, 5, 8, 9, 11, and 12 argue against allowing homeschoolers to play. Number 8 presents an option for logical argument.

B. "Ban Those Books"

Paragraph 1:

- argument *ad populum* (use of scare tactics: "very existence . . . is threatened")
- either/or fallacy ("cleanse or reconcile ourselves")

Paragraph 2:

- hypostatization ("History has shown")
- begging the question ("immoral books," "Communist plot")
- argument *ad hominem* ("liberal free-thinkers and radicals" are threatening names to some people)
- *post hoc* (the number of cut classes and the decline in the number of seniors going on to college were not necessarily caused by placing the books in the library that year)

Paragraph 3:

- either/or fallacy ("natural decline . . . or the influence of those dirty books")
- *non sequitur* (obviously, other reasons can exist for the changes in the students' behavior)
- begging the question ("dirty books," "undesirable characters")
- argument *ad populum* ("innocent children")

61

Paragraph 4:

- argument *ad populum* ("simple man . . . farm boy" versus the "pseudointellectuals," "Communist conspiracy," "good folks")
- bandwagon appeal (all the "right-thinking neighbors")

Assignment, p. 301

Answers will vary.

■ Discussion, Answers to Questions, Vocabulary

USA Today: "Four Is Not Enough" and Gary A. Schmidt's "Opposing View: We Like the Four-Day Week"—p. 306

Discussion

These two essays debate the value of changing the public school week from a traditional five-day schedule to a four-day week. Although some students may at first enthusiastically endorse the shorter school week, they should be cautioned to look at the two essays in terms of their persuasiveness. To emphasize the importance of audience awareness in argument, teachers might set up small groups and ask each one to assess the essays from the point of view of particular people: parents, teachers, administrators, students who hold after-school jobs or attend sports practices, school board members, and so on. Which arguments are the most persuasive to each audience, and why? (Students who have participated in a shortened school week schedule may have strong opinions to share with their classmates as well.)

Answers to Questions, p. 308

1. School districts throughout the country are considering changing their academic schedules to reduce expenses during our nation's economic downturn. School districts in seventeen states have reduced the school week from five days to four days in order to trim their budgets.
2. *USA Today* maintains that a shorter school week may reduce financial costs, but will cost the country more in lost educational opportunities in the future. On the other hand, Schmidt believes that the change is beneficial to his students and staff. He states that morale has increased, student and staff absences have been reduced, student achievement has not been compromised, and the district saves thousands of dollars per day.
3. Their primary objection is that students will receive less instructional time and learning will be reduced.
4. The editors cite the Massachusetts schools, the Brookings Institution, and the Southern Regional Board of Education to lend credibility to their arguments against a four-day week. These citations offer evidence that a shorter week is detrimental to student learning and financial savings are minimal.
5. These questions raise additional arguments against the four-day school week by suggesting hypothetical problems..
6. The MACCRAY superintendent claims that his system's test scores have not been affected, but the editorial board states that MACCRAY's math and reading scores are below the state average. The editors are persuading the audience by attacking one of MACCRAY's arguments supporting the shortened week.
7. Schmidt claims that the shortened week has actually added instructional time, saves money, and will not affect students' academic instruction.
8. Schmidt's discussion of the district's predecision research would be strengthened by including specific statistics, examples, and quotes.

9. Schmidt explains that a shorter week will not shorten learning time. Instead, he argues that students will have more instructional time in a shorter week because there will be fewer breaks for recess and lunch and less time between classes.
10. Student answers will vary, though Schmidt's essay is weaker overall. See the suggestions for small-group work described on p. 62.

Vocabulary

USA Today essay:

1. innovative (2)—tending to innovate or characterized by innovation
2. latch-key children (2)—refers to children who return from school to an empty home because the parents are at work
3. rationale (3)—the fundamental reason serving to account for something
4. conversions (6)—change in character, form, or function

Schmidt's essay:

1. standardized (2)—to compare with or test by a standard
2. unanticipated (2)—unexpected or not anticipated
3. morale (2)—emotional or mental condition with respect to cheerfulness, confidence, zeal
4. instructional (3)—the act or practice of teaching; education
5. solicit (6)—to seek or ask for

■ Analyzing Advertisements, p. 309

Conflicting Positions: Gun Control, p. 309

Discussion

Student responses to these advertisements will vary. Instructors might use discussion of these advertisements to emphasize that one's personal beliefs about gun control and the safe use of energy should not make the reader blind to the various appeals—both effective and flawed—that the advertisements employ. Some of the appeals used are listed below.

N.R.A. advertisement gives biographical details that present Gutman as a successful business and civic leader and family-oriented man and emphasizes his experiences in communist Cuba and the Florida legislature to add authority to his support for the N.R.A., thus perhaps strengthening the credibility of the N.R.A. for the reader. Students can debate the overall effectiveness of one example in support of a large cause.

The "Well-Regulated Militia" advertisement: emphasizes the contrast between "self-styled 'citizen militias'" that cite the Second Amendment as support for their weapons and military training and the National Guard, which the ad states is the true militia protected by the Second Amendment (the photo of the militia group plays on reader emotions); Supreme Court justice Warren Burger's views are quoted (appealing to reader's regard for intellectual authority) to strengthen the advertisement's claim that the Second Amendment does not prohibit gun-control laws.

The Right to Bears and Arms advertisement: emphasizes the number of deaths associated with guns while suggesting that guns have fewer manufacturing regulations than teddy bears. Appeals largely to emotions centered on children and implicates gun manufacturers heavily in the accidental deaths of children.

Competing Products: Sources of Energy, p. 313

Discussion

In these three ads, students will have various responses to the visual appeals and effectiveness, but the arguments can be viewed as fairly straightforward.

Metropolitan Energy Council, Inc. advertisement: the emotional appeals here are to fear and protection of loved ones, especially children—an *ad populum* argument for parents (a mother and her toddler are pictured) that focuses on the danger of gas heat, a belief that is based on no concrete evidence (at least in the ad). The ad also insinuates that because the gas companies are large, they are also, impersonal, a non sequitur, and because of this they don't care about their customers and are therefore negligent. This is a red herring and has no basis in fact.

Xcel Energy advertisement: this ad tries to educate the consumer about gas smells and what to do in case of a leak. It also appeals to intellect and to protection of loved ones, but in this case the latter is a direct response to the concerns in the previous ad. Running an ad that appears to be a public safety announcement makes the company appear caring and concerned for the welfare of the public, much in the way parents would be for their children.

U.S. Council for Energy Awareness advertisement: a largely emotional appeal centered on the photo of a baby sea turtle. It emphasizes the environmental safety of nuclear energy by implying that it has less negative impact on endangered species and fragile ecosystems than other energy sources. This ad argues against oil and gas as pollutants. It appeals to protection of children and the environment via the baby turtle, but it begs the question of whether or not nuclear energy is safe.

Popular Appeals: Spending Our Money, p. 317

Discussion

The "American Values" ad tries to persuade people that if the founder has down-to-earth values and frugal ways (brings an inexpensive peanut butter sandwich to the employees' cafeteria; reuses paper sack), then the company is trustworthy, reliable, and successful. There is, of course, no correlation between what the founder eats for lunch and the company's business practices.

Pierce Brosnan's ad offers a "bandwagon" appeal to customers who wish to imitate, through their accessories, the rugged-but-suave demeanor of James Bond and other adventurous characters this actor has played. The watch's name is also chosen to connote strength and power ("—master") on both land ("Terra") and sea ("Aqua").

The PETA ad also uses the bandwagon appeal, this time in the guise of the beautiful and talented actress Charlize Theron. This ad also offers an excellent opportunity to discuss the persuasiveness (or lack of it) of analogy. Some students will agree with PETA that all animals should be treated as humanely as our pets; others will perhaps argue a distinction between domestic pets (e.g., dogs, cats) enjoyed for companionship and farmed animals (e.g., minks, cows, chickens) raised for production of fur, hides, food, etc.

Practicing What You've Learned, p. 321

The 1920s were years of great prosperity in this country, and this ad would have appealed to men who wish to demonstrate their wealth (and their "modern" views) by buying a car for their wife; adding a second car to the family was a luxury purchase at that time. This ad would also have appealed to the young women of this era who were breaking out of traditional female roles by driving cars, wearing make-up, playing sports, cutting their hair and hemlines short, etc. Students may contrast the appeals of this ad to auto/truck ads today; are there still ads that appeal along class or gender lines? (Consider, for example, "snob" appeal ads of sports cars or tough "macho" truck ads.)

Chapter 11
Description, p. 323

■ Summary

How to Write Effective Description
- recognize your purpose
- describe clearly, using specific details—select only appropriate details
- make your descriptions vivid

Problems to Avoid
- remember your audience
- avoid an erratic organization of details
- avoid any sudden change in perspective

Practicing What You've Learned, p. 328

A. Dillard watches the snake with fascination and admiration, referring to the snake's body as "perfect, whole, unblemished" (3). However, she is also cautious, as noted by the brief reference to her snake bite kit and the stomps on the ground before she is seated. Her description contains some objective details ("twelve or thirteen inches long," thick body, brown bands), but it is her subjective, figurative language that communicates her feelings toward the snake. Students may point to such images as "head …blunt as a stone ax," "low-forehead glare and lipless reptile smirk," "glass eyes of a stuffed warbler," among many other sensory details.

B. Responses will vary.

C. Responses will vary.

Assignment, p. 330

Responses will vary.

Essay Topics

A Topic Proposal for Your Essay
- identify your subject and whether you will describe it objectively or subjectively
- state at least one reason why you chose this topic
- identify your audience
- state your purpose and the effect you want to have on the reader
- list at least three details that will help clarify your subject
- identify difficulties that might arise during drafting

Sample Student Essay

Professional Essay

Questions on Content, Structure and Style

Suggestions for Writing

Vocabulary

A Revision Worksheet

Collaborative Activity

Reviewing Your Progress

■ Discussion, Answers to Questions, Vocabulary

"Still Learning from My Mother" by Cliff Schneider—p. 337

Discussion

Students might be encouraged to view this essay from a variety of perspectives, an idea that echoes Schneider's purpose as he brings in detail from a variety of memories and from comments made to him about his mother. This piece is reminiscent of the "my hero" or "my favorite role model" essay, but Schneider's details and focus draw the reader into this short description that invites the reader to glimpse life from multiple viewpoints of time, gender, values, and relationships.

Answers to Questions, p. 338

1. Text is primarily subjective as he describes his personal memories: "She never showed motherly concern, just a broad grin with the tip of her tongue exposed . . ." (1); "we'd notice this gleam in her eye" (2). Students will see others.
2. In 1950, most American mothers were housewives and homemakers whose primary domain was domestic, not athletic. Title IX called for education in athletics for all students, including women, and thus changed the face of sports and women's lives dramatically in the latter half of the twentieth century. Prior to this amendment, however, while women did participate in athletics, very few were prominent in the public eye and fewer still would have participated in them in conjunction with their role as "mother."
3. The dominant impression Schneider leaves us with is of a woman who takes joy in athletic competition. Details provided are plentiful: "grabs a glove" (1); "lettered in field hockey . . . gleam in her eye . . . ready for action . . . to have some fun . . . played hard, laughed a lot . . ." (2); "protests [her 8-pound bowling ball] is too light and doesn't give enough pin action" (3); "This is the year I'm going to bowl a 200 game" (4); etc. Students will find such details throughout.
4. "She would happily grab a glove, run out to the road and then fire fast balls at me that cracked my glove . . ." (1); "She never showed motherly concern, just a broad grin with the tip of her tongue exposed . . ." (1); "we'd notice this gleam in her eye" (2). She has class because "win or lose, she was always gracious" (2).
5. The description appeals to the physical sensation in such a way that the reader can almost feel the sting. Sensory detail promotes a physical response in the reader, not merely an intellectual nod of comprehension.
6. Her "perennial battle cry" reveals her as competitive, vivacious, goal oriented, and compelled to win, to achieve her best. Students may not be familiar with Vince Lombardi whose most famous quote is "Winning isn't everything; it's the only thing," which has been used to inspire male athletes and businessmen for over fifty years.
7. Dialogue provides direct evidence of personality but when Schneider quotes a neighbor, he reveals a public perception of his mother that helps to support his own respect and reverence for her athletic ability. Such dialogue furthers his purpose for describing his mother's perseverance toward a goal.

66

8. The organization is chronological and allows the reader to view the character historically, showing her zest for competition and athleticism as part of her personality and not simply as a trendy adaptation or hobby-like recreation.

9. Schneider learns how to compete graciously, to play hard, to have fun, but mostly that he can still learn from her and that one is "never too old to dream and . . . to realize those dreams." The title of the essay helps to immediately establish Schneider's purpose. His goal is to show that learning needn't always be viewed in an educational setting and that it can be gained from unexpected sources. While we often consider mothers as teachers, in this case the stereotype is broken. This role reversal may provide a place to redirect discussion toward expectations in reading, biased thinking, or deconstruction of gender stereotypes. Reading this essay in conjunction with Heilbroner's in the following chapter will provide additional perspectives and writing opportunities for students.

10. Yes, though for additional practice students might be asked to find places for action verbs or colorful adjectives.

Vocabulary

1. Title IX (2)—One of the Education Amendments of 1972—prohibited discrimination based on sex
2. diminished (3)—weakened; reduced
3. octogenarian (3)—a person in his or her 80s
4. concession (3)—something one concedes or gives up
5. toted (3)—carried
6. perennial (4)—returning seasonally; ongoing

Chapter 12
Narration, p. 343

■ Summary

Extended Versus Brief Narratives

Writing the Effective Narrative Essay

- know your purpose
- make your main point clear
- follow a logical time sequence
- use sensory details to hold the reader's interest
- make your characters believable/authentic
- use dialogue realistically

Problems to Avoid

- choose your subject carefully
- limit your scope
- don't let your story lag with insignificant detail

Practicing What You've Learned, p. 346

Responses will vary, but students will likely comment on the train-like sound of the tornado, the cries of the baby and the children, the smells of dirt and animals, and firm, fearful, or calm tones of voices.

Collaborative Activity

Answers will vary.

Essay Topics

A Topic Proposal for Your Essay

- state the subject of your narrative
- state why you selected this narrative
- identify your audience
- identify your purpose, desired effect
- summarize in a few descriptive words the critical moment of your story
- identify potential difficulties in writing this narrative

Sample Student Essay

Professional Essay

Questions on Content, Structure, and Style

Suggestions for Writing

Vocabulary

A Revision Worksheet

Collaborative Activity

Reviewing Your Progress

"Salvation" by Langston Hughes—p. 352

Discussion

Rather than become entangled in discussions about religious conversion, teachers might focus on the near-universal experience Hughes describes here: succumbing to pressure from friends, family, or community. Most people can identify with Hughes' conflict, whether in their lives they gave in or resisted on a particular occasion. Hughes' use of detail and dialogue gives his narrative movement and help readers feel present as the story unfolds. Hughes' vivid language may suggest ways students can capture a memorable moment in narrative essays of their own.

Answers to Questions, p. 353

1. Hughes' main purpose is to show for the remorse he felt for lying about his salvation and the subsequent mourning of his loss of religious faith.
2. Hughes sets the scene of the revival meeting with strong sensory details. Through Hughes' details, the reader can almost feel the smooth planks of the mourning bench and experience Hughes' discomfort as he remains on the bench. Details such as "a wonderful, rhythmical sermon, all moans and shouts and lonely cries and dire pictures of hell" and the images of "old women with jet-black faces and braided hair, old men with work-gnarled hands" transport the reader to the "hot, crowded church."
3. Hughes' aunt, the preacher, and various church members all pressure Hughes to be "saved."
4. Hughes resists going to the altar because he is waiting to actually see Jesus and experience the moment of salvation the way he had come to expect it to happen. He is conflicted because the church members continue to pressure him and the night is growing long.
5. Hughes' use of dialogue adds authenticity to the narrative. The preacher, the aunt, and Westley all speak directly to Hughes. The intensity of the preacher and aunt's words, as well as the resigned tone of Westley's words, give the reader a sense of the pressure Hughes felt.
6. Like Hughes, Westley had lingered on the mourner's bench, and, like Hughes, Westley does not "see Jesus"; however, he succumbs to the preacher's pressure and climbs up the platform. Hughes emphasizes Westley's actions because they foreshadow his own. Once Hughes sees that Westley is not punished for lying in church, Hughes' faith dissolves and he too climbs up the platform.
7. Hughes finally joins the other children on the platform because he is growing weary of the adults' pleas and cries. He also feels some guilt for "holding everything up so long."
8. Figurative language is important to the story because it allows the reader to fully understand Hughes' experience. When reading the phrases "a sea of shouting" and "waves of rejoicing," the reader understands that Hughes felt like he was being swept away by the emotion and intensity of the moment, much like the drag and pull of the ocean tide.
9. Hughes is crying because he has lied and lost his faith in Jesus. Ironically, the aunt interprets his crying as tears of joy for having "found Jesus."
10. Student responses will vary.

Vocabulary

1. revival (1)—a church meeting often for the purpose of reawakening religious faith
2. dire (3)—urgent or desperate
3. deacons (6)—an appointed or elected church officer
4. serenely (7)—calmly, peacefully, or tranquilly
5. knickerbockered (11)—wearing short pants or knickers

Chapter 13
Essays Using Multiple Strategies, p. 357

■ Summary

Multiple Strategy Responses
- strategies are seldom used in isolation
- strategies are various ways to think about a topic
- strategies serve a specific purpose

Choosing the Best Strategies
- questions to help select strategies to match your purpose

Problems to Avoid
- overkill; using all strategies
- illogical organization

Practicing What You've Learned

Student responses will vary.

Sample Student Essay

Professional Essay

Questions on Content, Structure, and Style

Suggestions for Writing

Vocabulary

A Revision Worksheet

Collaborative Activity

Reviewing Your Progress

■ Discussion, Answers to Questions, Vocabulary

"Don't Let Stereotypes Warp Your Judgments" by Robert L. Heilbroner—p. 363

Discussion

Students can readily identify with this essay by listing on the board a variety of stereotypes they have experienced either by having judged or by having been judged by others. If they were going to write a similar essay or respond to this one, what specific examples from their experience could they offer? After this discussion, use question 10 below (identifying the different strategies Heilbroner uses) as the basis for a group activity. Divide students into groups and have them list the strategies in the essay and tell why the author has used each at a specific point in the essay. Each group can explain a few paragraphs in a feedback session after this group work.

Answers to Questions, p. 366

1. Heilbroner uses these questions to call up common stereotypes most readers will share in order to connect readers to the practice of prejudging people. If he were to begin differently, with a definition of prejudice, for example, readers might immediately react that they certainly are not prejudiced. The examples will help readers see they all share some of these sometimes subtle stereotypes.

2. Heilbroner defines a stereotype as "a kind of gossip about the world" that is the basis of prejudice. The studies illustrate that stereotyping is a subconscious, ever-present influence on our perceptions and beliefs.

3. Using first person includes Heilbroner in "those who stereotype" and, by this admission, connects him more closely to the readers who are also a part of "we." By doing so, the essay becomes more of an easily accepted observation on a tendency of human nature rather than a scolding lecture such as "You should not prejudge others."

4. One of the reasons stereotypes develop is that as children we begin "type casting" people, sorting out the "good guys" and the "bad guys." Also, the media perpetuates stereotypes in jokes, characterizations, and advertising. We stereotype to make sense of the confusion of our world, to give definition to the chaos around us.

5. One who stereotypes loses the opportunity to create an individual picture of the world. By seeing the world as so many categories of identical "cutouts" instead of seeing it as diverse and nuanced, the person becomes a stereotype who is totally predictable and inflexible.

6. Heilbroner's opening examples are hypothetical (see answer 1). The specific examples from the studies add concrete support to his claim about the ubiquitous nature of stereotyping. In paragraph 11, the author cites two commonly held stereotypes to explain how we rationalize and confirm our prejudices. Other groups of frequently held stereotypes found in paragraphs 12 and 15 help a reader begin to recognize and question those beliefs.

7. The three-step process in paragraphs 18–20 outlines a way readers can acknowledge complexity and individuality rather than perpetuate stereotypes.

8. These quotations lend authority and broad support to Heilbroner's statements.

9. The conclusion underscores what the reader has to gain from the essay. The metaphor of paintings in a gallery is a memorable way for the reader to go away with a strong grasp of the overall process of stereotyping; the metaphor condenses the process into a vivid mental picture.

10. Strategies used in the essay:
    Paragraphs 1–3 Hypothetical examples
    Paragraph 4 Specific examples
    Paragraph 5 Definition
    Paragraph 6 Specific examples
    Paragraphs 7–13 Causal analysis
    Paragraphs 15–19 Process analysis

Vocabulary

1. swarthy (4)—dark complexioned
2. dinned (8)—told repeatedly and persistently
3. perpetuated (8)—continued indefinitely
4. synchronized (9)—regulated the timing of
5. semantics (11)—study of the relationship between words and their meanings
6. vindicated (11)—cleared from suspicion or guilt
7. impoverish (12)—to make poor
8. chastening (18)—correcting
9. edifice (18)—an imposing building
10. chary (19)—cautious, wary

71

Part 3
Special Assignments

Chapter 14
Writing a Paper Using Research, p. 371

■ Summary

Focusing Your Topic
- some are assigned and already specific and narrowed
- others are more general and need a little or a lot of narrowing

Beginning Your Library Research
- general reference works
- online catalogs
- databases
- the Internet
- special collections

Conducting Primary Research
- collect first-hand data to obtain information not available from other sources
- interview
- use questionnaires

The Personal Interview

Conducting the Personal Interview

Before the interview
- know your purpose
- make an appointment
- educate yourself about your topic
- plan some questions

During the interview
- make a good first impression
- ask, listen, ask
- be flexible
- ask for more details when necessary and use a friendly tone
- keep to the original topic, when necessary redirect discussion
- conclude thoughtfully and thank the interviewee

After the interview
- review your notes immediately
- consider sending a copy of your work to the interviewee
- send a thank-you note

The Questionnaire

Developing the Questionnaire

- know your purpose and target audience
- encourage participation
- choose the most effective type of questionnaire
- yes/no answers
- multiple choice
- checklist
- rank order
- rating system
- open questions
- watch your language
- clarify vague references and abbreviations
- avoid loaded questions
- focus on one piece of information per question
- keep it short, simple, and smooth

Administering the Questionnaire

- secure a valid sampling
- perform a test run
- prepare ahead—distribution, collection, permissions, materials

Totaling and Reporting the Results

- analyze responses
- report findings accurately

Preparing a Working Bibliography

- things to note from sources

Choosing and Evaluating Your Sources

The writer should ask:
- What do I know about the author?
- What do I know about the publisher?
- Is my research reasonably balanced? Is the site unbiased?
- Are my sources reporting valid research?
- Are my sources still current?

Preparing an Annotated Bibliography

[Note: Requiring students to compile an annotated bibliography at this stage of the research process may be an effective way of ensuring progress is being made. This might help writers avoid the weak research sources so often found in a frenzied last-minute search.]

Taking Notes

- use index cards—easily organized, research notebook, or computer file
- use photocopies—title pages and bibliographic information with page numbers
- use computer note files—easily transferred into essay draft
- direct quotations
- paraphrase
- summary
- your own ideas

Distinguishing Paraphrase from Summary
- paraphrase: puts information in researcher's own words, follows order of original text, and includes important details
- summary: uses key ideas, omits supporting details, and is much shorter than original

Incorporating Your Source Material
- use your sources in a clear, logical way
- don't overuse direct quotations
- don't "drop in" direct quotations next to your prose
- vary your sentence pattern when you present quotations
- punctuate your quotations correctly
- make certain your support is in your paper
- don't let reference material dominate your essay

Avoiding Plagiarism
Practicing What You've Learned

Assignment

Collaborative Activity

Choosing the Documentation Style for Your Essay

MLA Style
- MLA citations in your essay
- compiling a Works Cited list
- sample entries
- electronic sources

APA Style
- APA citations in your essay
- compiling a reference list
- sample entries
- electronic sources

Special Note: The description of the title page for APA essays (page 415) has been modified for academic essays (course name, section number, instructor's name). For papers submitted for professional publication, APA style recommends a title page with the work's name, the author's name, the school's name, and, if appropriate, an "Author's Note" containing any additional information such as college/department affiliation, acknowledgment of any research support (grants, fellowships, etc.), and the author's postal and/or e-mail address. In all cases, writers using APA style should follow guidelines set by the publication to which they are submitting their work.

Footnote/Bibliography Form
Practicing What You've Learned

Collaborative Activity

Using Supplementary Notes

Sample Student Paper Using MLA Style

Student Sample Using APA Style

■ Answers to "Practicing What You've Learned" Exercises

Practicing What You've Learned, p. 399

A. 1. Bibliography Card

Marien, Mary Warner and Fleming, William. *Fleming's Arts & Ideas*. 10. Boston: Wadsworth/Cengage Learning, 2005. Print. Notes from 585-586.

   2. Paraphrase

Frida Kahlo was a Mexican artist linked by some critics to the Surrealists. According to Marien and Fleming, her art was inspired by her life, especially a painful accident that left her crippled (585).

   3. Summary

Frida Kahlo, a Mexican painter and muralist, painted scenes inspired by painful moments in her own life. The painting *Self-Portrait with Thorn Necklace and Hummingbird* illustrates the pain she felt after her divorce from Diego Rivera.

   4. In *Fleming's Arts and Ideas*, Marien and Fleming explain that Kahlo "drew directly on the events in her life, particularly the accident that left her partly crippled and in pain " (585-586).

   5. Kahlo's work also focuses on lost love. In her painting *Self-Portrait with Thorn Necklace and Hummingbird*, the hummingbird "refers to her recent divorce from muralist Diego Rivera, whom she soon remarried" (Marien and Fleming 586).

B. Answers will vary.

Assignment

A. Answers will vary.
B. Answers will vary.

Practicing What You've Learned, p. 422

Answers will vary.

Chapter 15
Writing in Class: Exams and "Response" Essays, p. 441

■ Summary

Steps to Writing Well Under Pressure

1. Clarify for yourself the kind of task you face.
   - "short answer" exam questions
   - essay exam questions
   - "prompted" essays
   - summary-and-response essays
2. Arrive prepared.
   - bring essential materials such as paper, extra pens and pencils, a stopwatch
   - be courteous to your classmates
3. Read the assignment with great care.
4. Prepare to write.
   - think positively
   - take the first few minutes to think and plan
   - after choosing a thesis jot down a brief plan or outline
   - budget your time before beginning to write
5. Begin writing, remembering what you have learned about paragraphing, topic sentences, and supporting evidence.
   - write on only one side of the paper
   - try to conclude your essay in a satisfactory way
6. If time allows, read what you have written.
7. Put your name on every page.

Problems to Avoid

- misreading the assignment
- incomplete essay/exam
- composition amnesia
- gorilla generalizations

Practicing What You've Learned

Assignment

Writing the Summary-and-Response Essay

Reading the Assignment and the Article

- determine what you are being asked to do
- thoroughly understand the ideas in the assigned reading
- study and annotate articles if given the opportunity ahead of time

Writing the Summary Section

- treat the article's ideas objectively
- include the author's name and the title of the article
- paraphrase

Writing the Response Section

- check your notes
- determine your overall assessment
- plan your organization
- transition smoothly between sections
- use tag lines
- use supporting evidence
- include a critique of author's logic, style, or tone if allowed
- conclude consistently with your overall assessment

Sample Student Essay

Practicing What You've Learned

Collaborative Activity

Assignment

■ Answers to "Practicing What You've Learned" Exercises

Practicing What You've Learned, p. 448

1. Underline "flower imagery" and "major themes . . . The Bluest Eye." Circle "Discuss," "examples," and "clarify." Example, causal analysis, or argument.
2. Underline "the Bay of Pigs . . . Cuba." Circle "Trace" and "the events that led to." Causal analysis, process; description.
3. Underline "Louis B. Mayer" and "American Film . . . of Moviemaking." Circle "Discuss" and "major influences on." Causal analysis, description, argument.
4. Underline "The 1957 . . . system." Circle "Agree or disagree." Argument.
5. Underline "expressionistic techniques" of…Jaune Quick-to-See Smith and Audrey Flack." Circle "similarities and differences" and "Illustrate." Compare/contrast, example.

Assignment, p. 448

Student responses will vary.

Practicing What You've Learned, p. 453

A. Student responses will vary.
B. Student responses will vary.

Assignment, p. 454

Student responses will vary.

Chapter 16
Writing about Literature, p. 455

■ Summary

Using Literature in the Composition Classroom
- prompts: using literature as a springboard for an essay
- literary analysis: interpretation of a piece of literature

Suggestions for Close Reading of Literature
- read and reread
- annotate
- dispel myth about "hidden meanings"
- seek ways to reasonably support your own interpretation

Steps to Reading a Story
- check biographical information
- read the title and consider what it may reveal about the story
- read story once for plot
- look up important vocabulary words
- make preliminary notes on major themes
- analyze story's parts and reason for each; evaluate point of view
- analyze structure of story
- analyze characters
- examine setting and its import
- study language use: figurative language, symbols, style, and tone
- review and refine initial reactions

Annotated Story

Sample Student Essay

Steps to Reading a Poem
- check biographical information
- read the title and consider what it may reveal about the poem
- read poem at least twice; paraphrase poem; analyze sentences and vocabulary
- decide if poem is narrative or lyrical; determine dominant idea
- analyze narrator of poem
- examine the setting or occasion of poem
- analyze characters
- examine the poem's word choice
- analyze the structure of the poem
- examine the sound devices
- analyze the rhythm
- review and refine initial reactions

Annotated Poem

Sample Student Essay

Guidelines for Writing about Literature

- ■ select a workable topic
- ■ present a clear thesis
- ■ follow literary conventions
- ■ organize effectively
- ■ use ample evidence
- ■ find a pleasing conclusion

Problems to Avoid

- ■ don't assign meanings; show evidence of your interpretation
- ■ don't drop in quoted lines without explaining them
- ■ don't rehash the plot in summary; don't neglect analysis

Practicing What You've Learned

Suggestions for Writing

■ Answers to "Practicing What You've Learned" Exercises

Practicing What You've Learned, p. 473

"Geraldo No Last Name" by Sandra Cisneros

In this excerpt, Cisneros challenges readers to see the tragedy of stereotyping and misunderstanding in an often-impersonal world. Geraldo is regarded as a poor nobody; no one much cares. Had the hospital been better staffed (and more concerned?), he might have been saved or at least properly identified. Even Marin, who hardly knows him but cared enough to spend hours at the hospital, is encouraged to move on—after all, he was just another illegal immigrant. No one understood how hard he worked, living frugally and sending money home. Sadly, Geraldo is even misunderstood after death: his family never learned his fate and thinks he simply abandoned them. The lack of a last name universalizes Geraldo; he could be any one of us. (This story might be usefully paired with Robert Heilbroner's essay "Don't Let Stereotypes Warp Your Judgments," which appears in Chapter 13.)

Practicing What You've Learned, p. 475

"The Cask of Amontillado" by Edgar Allan Poe

In "The Cask of Amontillado," Poe's narrator is speaking to someone who "knows his soul so well," and thus, since he is also telling the tale from the perspective of events that happened in the past, we might assume he is confessing to his priest, perhaps on his own deathbed, as it is a "half-century" that has passed that "no mortal" has disturbed the pile of bones he replaced in front of Fortunato's grave. Readers may debate whether Montresor is a reliable narrator or whether he is lying about, fantasizing, or exaggerating his story of revenge. Is he sane or mad? Has he punished without guilt? Some students may be reminded that Poe was America's first master of horror (not Stephen King!) and that this 1846 story helped define the genre. To illustrate the way Poe created this macabre story, teachers might divide the class into groups and assign each one a topic to explore: point of view, sensory detail (sight, sound, touch), irony and word play, characterization of Montresor and Fortunato. How do all these elements work together to present the story's dominant effect?

80

"Those Winter Sundays" by Robert Hayden and "The Road Not Taken" by Robert Frost

The point of view in both of these poems is first person. Frost's speaker assumes he will look back on his action in later years, while Hayden's speaker seems new to understanding the father's behavior when the speaker was a child. This understanding may have come after the father has died or because the speaker has become a parent. Hayden describes the father's work and attention to his family's needs. Frost describes choosing a path in life, one that has "made all the difference" to him. Hayden's language is cold and hard where there is misunderstanding in the speaker's perspective—"*blueblack cold*," "*crac*ked hands," "*c*old splin*t*ering," "brea*k*ing," and "*ch*ronic anger." In contrast, the imagery softens with the smoother sound of "*love's austere* and *lonely offices*" in the speaker's retrospective comprehension of parental love and duty.

Frost's roads as a metaphor for life's choices suggests that the path that most choose is safe but perhaps not as meaningful or adventurous. Neither are "trodden black" nor unworthy choices, but once either is followed, returning to the same moment/place of choice will not likely happen.

Chapter 17
Writing about Visual Arts, p. 485

■ Summary

- artistic visual images enrich our lives
- we learn to analyze through writing
- we need to scrutinize visual images

Using Visual Arts in the Composition Classroom

- personal response
- formal analysis
- strategy practice
- prompted response

Suggestions for Analyzing Paintings

- prepare for your viewing
- note first impressions
- record basic information
- study the subject matter
- scenes with one or more figures
- a portrait
- a landscape
- a still life
- nonrepresentational art
- beyond realism
- analyze composition and design
- arrangement of subject matter/focal point
- balance of subject matter
- symbolism
- light and shadow
- colors and effects
- lines and shape—regularity
- medium used
- brush strokes
- pigmentation
- texture
- identify period style or "school"

Additional Advice about Sculpture and Photography

Sculptures

- form—time and place
- subject type
- cultural expression
- pose

- materials
- angles of view
- placement, positioning, environment

Photography

- purpose
- name of photographer, photo, subject matter, place and date of photo, place of publication or exhibition
- composition and circumstances or methods used to affect a response
- lighting
- color or the absence of
- exposure time
- depth of field
- angle and range of vision
- focus
- arrangement of subject matter

Practicing What You've Learned

Collaborative Activity

Guidelines for Writing about Art Works

- use a catchy lead-in
- write a compelling thesis
- present an overview of the work
- organize main points effectively
- provide clear supporting evidence
- conclude gracefully

Problems to Avoid

- pay close attention to the assignment
- use vivid description to inform and delight

Annotated Painting: *Nighthawks*

Sample Student Essay

Suggestions for Writing

■ Answers to "Practicing What You've Learned" Exercises

Practicing What You've Learned, p. 497

A. Answers will vary.
B. Answers will vary.

Chapter 18
Writing about Film, p. 505

■ Summary

Using Film in the Composition Classroom
- prompted response
- review essay
- strategy practice
- formal analysis

Guidelines for Writing about Film
- pay close attention to your assignment
- prepare in advance of your first screening
- arrange multiple viewing opportunities
- take notes both as you watch and immediately after, while your memory is fresh
- review your notes in light of your assignment's purpose
- watch the film again with an analytical eye
- consider conventions used in writing about film
- use clear, precise language
- proofread for accuracy in details and mechanics, including citing sources

Problems to Avoid
- don't "pun and run"; explain your views
- don't allow a plot summary to dominate your discussion; have a purpose in mind

Sample Student Essay

Practicing What You've Learned

Collaborative Activity

Professional Essay

"Cinematic Riches in *Millionaire*" by Ty Burr--p. 514

A. Burr's film review clearly urges audiences to see the film *Slumdog Millionaire*. Burr cautions that this is not simply a sentimental, feel-good movie but one that also addresses abject poverty and violence. Even so, he maintains that audiences will be uplifted after seeing *Slumdog Millionaire* because of the archetypal characters, the well-developed plot, the "beautiful" music, the strong editing, and the powerful scenery. The inclusion of details teaches students the importance of strengthening their points with examples. Burr's colorful colloquial diction, sentence fragments, and snappy tone are worthwhile topics for discussion. Are his language choices and "voice" appropriate for his particular audience? Do students find his choices effective, distracting, or even annoying?

B. Answers will vary.

Suggestions for Writing

Glossary of Film Terms

Chapter 19
Writing in the World of Work, p. 521

■ Summary

Composing Business Letters

- determine the main purpose of this letter
- determine the audience. What should he/she know, understand, or decide to do after reading this letter?
- decide what impression of yourself you want to present

Business Letter Format

- heading
- inside address
- salutation
- text
- complimentary closing
- signature
- notes such as encl., cc, xc, c when appropriate
- avoid postscripts
- proofread

Practicing What You've Learned

Assignment

Sample Business Letter

Creating Memos

- a common form of brief communication within a business or organization
- clear and concise

Sending Professional E-mail

- use a helpful subject line
- begin with an appropriate greeting
- be brief
- ease eyestrain; keep paragraphs short and skip lines between
- use a polite, friendly tone and clear, precise words
- use a closing appropriate to the audience
- revise, proofread, copy, send

Problems to Avoid

- remember that business e-mail is not private
- don't shout by using all caps
- don't use abbreviations or emoticons
- don't forward other people's e-mail without permission
- think twice before you write

Designing Cover Letters and Résumés

- functional format places the reader's focus on the applicant's education and skills
- experiential format emphasizes work history
- include heading
- include employment objective
- include education history: schools, locations, majors, minors, date of degrees
- list professional experience
- note skills
- include honors, awards, activities
- provide references, persons to contact for more information

Critique Your Page Appeal

- use high-quality paper and laser print ink
- balance text and white space
- arrange material in an engaging way
- proofread

Problems to Avoid

- never lie
- contact your references in advance and thank them after in a note
- add personal information thoughtfully
- consider providing keywords (and simple formats, clear fonts) for scanning software

Sample Résumés

Practicing What You've Learned

Assignment

Collaborative Activity

Preparing Interview Notes and Post-Interview Letters

■ Answers to "Practicing What You've Learned" Exercises

Practicing What You've Learned, p. 526

Answers will vary.

Assignment, p. 526

Answers will vary.

Practicing What You've Learned, p. 538

Answers will vary.

Assignment, p. 538

Answers will vary. Students may note one another's grammatical errors and errors in diction. Students may also critique one another's font choices or page design and offer advice for creating professional-looking documents.

Part 4
A Concise Handbook

Chapter 20
Major Errors in Grammar, p. 549

■ Summary

Errors with Verbs

- faulty agreement

Practicing What You've Learned

- subjunctive
- tense shift
- split infinitive
- double negatives
- passive voice
- irregular verbs

Practicing What You've Learned

Errors with Nouns

- possessive with "-ing" nouns
- misuse of nouns as adjectives
- plurals of proper nouns

Errors with Pronouns

- faulty agreement
- vague reference
- shift in pronouns
- incorrect case
- incorrect compound forms

Practicing What You've Learned

Errors with Adverbs and Adjectives

- incorrect usage
- faulty comparison

Practicing What You've Learned

Errors in Modifying Phrases

- dangling modifiers
- misplaced modifiers

Practicing What You've Learned

Errors in Sentences

- fragments

Practicing What You've Learned
- run-on sentence

Practicing What You've Learned
- comma splice

Practicing What You've Learned

Assignment

Collaborative Activity
- faulty parallelism

Practicing What You've Learned
- false predication
- mixed structure

Practicing What You've Learned

■ Answers to "Practicing What You've Learned" Exercises

Errors with Verbs

Practicing What You've Learned, p. 551

A. 1. A recent report on Cuban land crabs <u>shows</u> they can run faster than horses.
2. The team from Snooker Hollow High School <u>is</u> considering switching from basketball to basket weaving because passing athletics <u>is</u> now required for graduation.
3. Neither of the students <u>knows</u> that both mystery writer Agatha Christie and inventor Thomas Edison <u>were</u> dyslexic.
4. Each of the twins <u>has</u> read about Joseph Priestley's contribution to the understanding of oxygen, but neither <u>was</u> aware that he also invented the pencil eraser.
5. Clarity in speech and writing <u>is</u> absolutely essential in the business world today.
6. Some scholars believe that the world's first money, in the form of coins, <u>was</u> made in Libya, a country that is now part of Turkey.
7. Bananas, rich in vitamins and low in fats, <u>are</u> rated the most popular fruit in America.
8. There <u>are</u> many children in this country who appreciate a big plate of hot grits, but none of the Hall children <u>likes</u> this Southern dish.
9. Either the Labrador Retriever or the Yorkshire Terrier <u>holds</u> the honor of being the most popular breed of dogs in the United States, <u>says</u> the American Kennel Club.
10. Many people <u>consider</u> Johnny Appleseed a mythical figure, but now two local historians, authors of a well-known book on the subject, <u>argue</u> that he was a real person named John Chapman.

Practicing What You've Learned, p. 554

A. 1. He could hardly wait to hear country music star Sue Flay sing her version of his favorite song, "I've Been Flushed from the Bathroom of Your Heart."
2. "If you were in Wyoming and couldn't hear the wind blowing, what would people call you?" asked Jethro. "Dead," replied his buddy Herman.
3. The Aztec ruler Montezuma believed that chocolate had magical powers and could act as an aphrodisiac.
4. Tammy's favorite band is Opie Gone Bad, so she always buys their concert tickets, even though she can't afford to.

89

5. The Fire Department is raising suspicions of arson following the burning of the new Chip and Dale Furniture Factory. (Or, "Following the burning of the new Chip and Dale Furniture Factory, the Fire Department is raising suspicions of arson.")

B. 1. I saw what she was hiding behind her back.
2. He came around here yesterday asking questions, but we're used to that.
3. Having forgotten the combination to the safe, the burglar quietly sneaked out the back door. ("Snuck" is dialectical.)
4. Austin doesn't like to be awakened until noon.
5. The kids did good work all day.

Errors with Nouns and Pronouns

Practicing What You've Learned, p. 559

A. 1. Please buy a copy of the book *The Celery Stalks at Midnight* for my sister and <u>me</u>.
2. Between you and <u>me</u>, some people define a Freudian slip as saying one thing but meaning your mother.
3. <u>Who</u> is the singer of the country song "You Can't Make a Heel Toe the Mark"?
4. Aunt Beulah makes better cookies than <u>I</u>.
5. <u>She and I</u> are going to the movies to see *Attack of the Killer Crabgrass*.
6. I'm giving my accordion to <u>whoever</u> is carrying a grudge against our new neighbors, the <u>Smiths</u>.
7. The Botox surprise party was given by Paige Turner, Justin Case, and <u>me</u>.
8. She is the kind of person for <u>whom</u> housework meant sweeping the room with a glance.
9. <u>She and he</u> are twins who are always finding <u>themselves</u> in financial trouble.
10. The judge of the ugly feet contest announced <u>himself</u> the winner.

B. 1. Clarence and <u>I</u> have an uncle who is so mean that he writes the name of the murderer on the first page of mystery novels that are passed around the family.
2. Correct.
3. It was a surprise to both Mary and <u>me</u> to learn that Switzerland didn't give women the right to vote until 1971.
4. Each of the young women in the Family Life class decided not to marry after <u>she</u> read that couples today have 2.3 children.
5. Jim Bob explained that the best way for Frankie to avoid his recurring nosebleeds was to stay out of his cousin's marital arguments.
6. Those of us who'd had the flu agreed that <u>one</u> can always get a doctor to return <u>one's</u> call more quickly if <u>one</u> gets in the shower; but let's keep this tip confidential between you and <u>me</u>.
7. The stranger gave the free movie tickets to Louise and <u>me</u> after he saw people standing in line to leave the theater.
8. The personnel director told <u>each</u> of the employees, most of whom opposed him, to signify <u>his</u> or <u>her</u> "no" vote by saying, "I resign."
9. <u>People</u> know <u>they're</u> in trouble when <u>their</u> salary undergoes a modification reduction adjustment of 50 percent.
10. One of the first movies to gross over one million dollars was *Tarzan of the Apes* (1932), starring Johnny Weismuller, a former Olympic star who became an actor. <u>Such a large profit</u> didn't happen often in the movie industry at that time. (Or, At that time, it was unusual for Olympic champions to become movie stars.

Errors with Adverbs and Adjectives

Practicing What You've Learned, p. 561

A. 1. After the optometrist pulled her eye tooth, Hortense didn't behave very <u>well</u> in the waiting room.
   2. Which is the <u>worse</u> food—liver or buttermilk?
   3. I didn't do <u>well</u> on my nature project because my bonsai sequoia tree grew <u>badly</u> in its tiny container.
   4. Don't forget to dress <u>warmly</u> for the Arctic Freestyle Race.
   5. Of the twins, Teensie is <u>taller</u> than Egore.
   6. Watching Joe Bob eat candied fruit flies made Jolene feel <u>really</u> ill, and his table manners did not make her feel <u>better</u>.
   7. The Roman toothpick holder was <u>unique</u>.
   8. That was the <u>funniest</u> flea circus I have ever seen.
   9. Does the instructional guide *Bobbing for Doughnuts* still sell <u>well</u>?
   10. The Fighting Mosquitoes were trained <u>well</u>, but they just didn't take practices <u>seriously</u>.

Errors in Modifying Phrases

Practicing What You've Learned, p. 563

1. After tasting the meals on Hard Luck Airlines, we decided to return home via ship.
2. To report a fire, please use the fire department's new phone number found on the enclosed sticker, which can be displayed prominently on your telephone.
3. The prize-winning sculptor celebrated her $10,000 purchase of a new open-air studio in Aspen, where she lives with her infant daughter.
4. Showing off letters strewn over his desk, the movie star noted they were all from admirers.
5. Running too fast during a game of "Kick the Can," I collided with the flagpole.
6. Eloise bought a computer with a faulty memory from her neighbor.
7. From her closet, Jean tossed the baggy, wrinkled, and hopelessly out-of-style skirt.
8. Forgetting to pack underwear, Jonas had to reopen his already bulging suitcase.
9. Next spring at Slippery Rock College, Blanche will teach a course that incorporates her research into the mating habits of Big Foot.
10. Discovering that Kate had spent all night in the library, her friends knew she would need a trip to Special Coffee.
11. Squeezing the can, Dee Dee thought the tomatoes weren't quite ripe.
12. For the first year of their lives, children don't require solid food.
13. He doubted the old bicycles would make it over the mountains.
14. I read in a book from the public library that a number of modern sailors, like Thor Heyerdahl, have sailed primitive vessels across the ocean.
15. By proofreading carefully, you can easily spot and correct dangling modifiers.

Fragment Sentence Errors

Practicing What You've Learned, p. 565

A. "It is true that" the following are fragments.
   1. Which was in the middle of the Great Depression when money was scarce.
   2. As recorded by the United Drive-in Theater Owners Association.
   3. Perhaps because escalating land prices make property too valuable for use in this way. Or the fact that they are only open during the summer months.
   4. Including the American territories, too.

91

5. For instance, the miniature golf industry, down from 50,000 courses in the 1930s to fewer than 15,000 today.

B. 1. According to Lawrence M. Ausbel, author of "Credit Cards" in *The McGraw-Hill Encyclopedia of Economics,* the idea of a credit card first appeared in 1887.
   2. Originally an imaginary concept in a futurist novel by Edward Bellamy, the card allowed characters to charge against future earnings.
   3. Around the turn of the century, some American stores issued paper or metal "shoppers' plates," although they were used only by retailers to identify their credit customers.
   4. The first real credit card was issued in 1947 by a New York bank and was a success, despite the fact that customers could charge purchases only in a two-block area in Brooklyn.
   5. Travel and entertainment cards soon appeared, including the American Express card in 1958 and Carte Blanche in 1959, which allowed customers to charge items and services across the country.

Run-on Sentence

Practicing What You've Learned, p. 566

   1. While workers in the United States take an average of thirteen days of vacation a year, in Italy they take forty-two.
   2. In 1901, a school teacher named Annie Edson Taylor became the first person to go over Niagara Falls in a wooden barrel; she is the only woman known to survive this risky adventure.
   3. Before the choir sang "Break Forth into Joy," the minister preached his farewell sermon.
   4. The first microwave oven marketed in 1959 was a built-in unit that cost a whopping $2,595.
   5. Coffee was considered a food in the Middle Ages, and travelers who found it growing in Ethiopia mixed it with animal fat.

Comma Splice Errors

Practicing What You've Learned, p. 567

A. 1. Most people know that the likeness of Susan B. Anthony appeared on an American dollar coin in the 1990s, but fewer people know exactly who she was or why she is so important.
   2. For most of her life Anthony fought for a woman's right to achieve the vote; she was an organizer of the world's first women's rights convention in 1848.
   3. Anthony often risked her safety and her freedom for her beliefs; she was arrested in 1872 for the crime of voting in an election.
   4. She also worked to secure laws to protect working women, whose wages at that time automatically belonged to their husbands.
   5. Unfortunately, Anthony did not live to see the 1920 passage of the Nineteenth Amendment that gave women the right to vote—she died in 1906.

B. 1. My mother is very politically conservative; she's written in George III for president in the last two elections.
   2. Mary Lou decided not to eat the alphabet soup because the letters spelled out "botulism."
   3. A dried gourd containing seeds probably functioned as the first baby rattle. Ancient Egyptian wall paintings show babies with such gourds clutched in their fingers.
   4. Opportunists who came to the South after the Civil War were often called "carpetbaggers" because they carried their belongings in cheaply produced travel bags made of Belgian carpet.
   5. A friend of mine offers a good definition of nasty theater critics on opening night. According to him, they're the people who can't wait to stone the first cast.

92

6. The Smithsonian Institution was started when English scientist James Smithson died in 1829 and willed his entire fortune to the United States to establish a foundation for knowledge.
7. The word "jack-o'-lantern" may have come from the legend of Irish Jack. A mean old man in life, he was condemned after death to wander the earth carrying a hollow turnip with a lump of burning coal inside.
8. People forget how large the blue whale is. It has a heart as large as a Volkswagen Beetle and can hold an elephant on its tongue.
9. Correct.
10. The famous Eiffel Tower, built for the 1889 Paris Exposition, has inspired many crazy stunts: in 1891, Silvain Domon climbed the 363 steps on stilts.

Assignment, p. 569

Answers will vary.

Errors in Parallelism

Practicing What You've Learned, p. 570

1. Is it true that Superman could leap tall buildings, run faster than a locomotive, and bounce bullets off his skin?
2. To celebrate the canned meat product called Spam, we attended the Texas Spamarama Festival to participate in the Spambalaya cook-off, the Spam-can toss, and the Spamjam Jazz session. Later, we danced to such favorites as "Twist and Snout."
3. My Aunt Clara swears she has seen Elvis snacking at the deli, browsing at the supermarket, munching at the pizza parlor, and reading in the cookbook section of the local bookstore.
4. According to my husband, summer air in Louisiana is 2 percent oxygen, 8 percent water, and 90 percent mosquitoes.
5. Many teachers believe that the most important keys to success for students in college include attending class, keeping up with reading, and being brave enough to ask questions. (Option: . . . *attending class, reading assigned material, and asking questions.*)
6. Yoga encourages its participants to work on increasing flexibility and strength while decreasing stress.
7. Drivers should eliminate distractions such as eating, drinking, using the cell phone, and changing radio stations.
8. Smart people learn from their own mistakes; smarter people learn from others' mistakes.
9. Theater class helped me to overcome shyness, to make new friends, and to engage confidently in other activities.
10. The writer Oscar Wilde, the dancer Isadora Duncan, the painter Max Ernst, and the rock star Jim Morrison are all buried in the same Paris cemetery.

Errors of False Predication and Mixed Structure

Practicing What You've Learned, p. 572

1. The team quarterback, A. M. Hall, who broke his finger and was sidelined last week for the Raiders' game, is expected to play in tonight's game.
2. The groom, a graduate of Centerville High School, has lived in Centerville all of his life.
3. On my way to the doctor's office, my car's universal joint went out, which caused me to steer into a tree, resulting in auto-body damage.

4. When he brought home a twenty-pound block of ice after ice fishing all day, he revealed his intelligence.
5. New residents with children should know that the town offers low-cost daycare services.
6. Nineteenth-century cynic Ambrose Bierce noted that marriage entails "a master, a mistress, and two slaves, making in all, two."
7. When the plumber shows up three hours late, I get mad.
8. I owe some of my success as an actor to my drama teacher.
9. Because sound travels slower than light, the advice parents give their teenagers should reach them about the time they turn forty.
10. He was found in a ditch near some stray cows when a passerby heard his cries for help.

Chapter 21
A Concise Guide to Punctuation, p. 573

■ Summary

The Period

The Question Mark

The Exclamation Point
Practicing What You've Learned

The Comma
Practicing What You've Learned

The Semicolon
Practicing What You've Learned

The Colon
Practicing What You've Learned

The Apostrophe
Practicing What You've Learned

Assignment

Collaborative Activity

Quotation Marks
Practicing What You've Learned

Parentheses

Brackets

The Dash
Practicing What You've Learned

The Hyphen
Practicing What You've Learned

Italics and Underlining
Practicing What You've Learned

Ellipsis Points

The Slash
Practicing What You've Learned

■ Answers to "Practicing What You've Learned" Exercises

Errors Using Periods, Question Marks, and Exclamation Points

Practicing What You've Learned, p. 574

1. The space program sent some cows into orbit last year. I think they are now known as the herd shot around the world.
2. Ms. Anita Bath wants to know why erasers never outlast their pencils.
3. Her French class at St. Claire's School on First Ave. was taught by Madame Beau V. Rhee, Ph.D.
4. Where do all the birds go when it's raining?
5. I have wonderful news! I won the lottery!

Comma Errors

Practicing What You've Learned, p. 579

A. 1. In 1886, temperance leader Harvey Wilcox left Kansas and purchased 120 acres near Los Angeles to develop a new town.
   2. Although there were no holly trees growing in that part of California, Mrs. Wilcox named the area Hollywood.
   3. Mrs. Wilcox may have named the place after a home owned by a friend living in Illinois.
   4. During the early years, settlers who shared the Wilcoxes' values moved to the area and banned the recreational drinking of alcoholic beverages. However, some alcohol consumption was allowed for medicinal purposes.
   5. Nevertheless, by 1910 the first film studio opened its doors inside a tavern on Sunset Boulevard. Within seven short years, the quiet community started by the Wilcoxes had vanished.

B. 1. Yes, Hortense, in the 1920s young women did indeed cut their hair, raise their hemlines, dab perfume behind their knees, and dance the Charleston.
   2. In 1873, Cornell University canceled the school's first intercollegiate football game with Michigan when the president announced, "I will not permit 30 men to travel 400 miles merely to agitate a bag of wind."
   3. Jane, Marian, Donna, Ann, and Cissy graduated from high school on June 5, 1964, in Texarkana, Texas, in the old Walnut Street Auditorium.
   4. "I may be a man of few opinions," said Henry, "but I insist that I am neither for nor against apathy."
   5. Did you know, for instance, that early American settlers once thought the tomato was so poisonous they only used the plant for decoration?

C. 1. The father decided to recapture his youth, so he took his son's car keys away.
   2. Although ice cream didn't appear in America until the 1700s, our country now leads the world in ice cream consumption; Australia is second, I think.
   3. Last summer, the large, friendly family that lives next door flew Discount Airlines and visited three cities on their vacation; however, their suitcases visited five.
   4. Researchers in Balboa, Panama, have discovered that the poisonous yellow-belly sea snake, which descended from the cobra, is the most deadly serpent in the world.
   5. Lulu Belle, my cousin, spent the week of September 1–7, 1986, in the woods near Dimebox, Texas, looking for additions to her extinct butterfly collection. However, she wasn't at all successful in her search.

96

Semicolon Errors

Practicing What You've Learned, p. 581

1. The soloist sang the well-known hymn "I Will Not Pass This Way Again" at her concert last night; the audience was delighted.
2. Apples have long been associated with romance. For example, one legend says if you throw an apple peel over your shoulder, it will fall into the shape of your true love's initial.
3. According to an 1863 book of etiquette, the perfect hostess will see to it that the works of male and female authors are properly separated on her bookshelves; however, if the authors happen to be married, their proximity may be tolerated.
4. Today, there are some 60,000 Americans older than 100; in 1960, there were only 3,222, according to *Health* magazine.
5. The sixth-grade drama club will present its interpretation of *Hamlet* tonight in the school cafeteria; all parents are invited to see this tragedy.
6. Some inventors who named weapons after themselves include Samuel Colt, the Colt revolver; Henry Deringer Jr., the derringer pistol; Dr. Richard Gatling, the crank machine gun: Col. John T. Thompson, the submachine or "tommy" gun; and Oliver F. Winchester, the repeating rifle.
7. My doctor failed in his career as a kidnapper; no one could read his ransom notes.
8. The highest point in the United States is Mt. McKinley at 20,320 feet; in contrast, the lowest point is Death Valley at 282 feet below sea level.
9. As we drove down the highway, we saw a sign that said "See the World's Largest Prairie Dog. Turn Right at This Exit"; therefore, we immediately stopped to look.
10. The next billboard read "See Live Jackalopes," making us want to stop again.

Errors with Colons

Practicing What You've Learned, p. 583

1. Experts have discovered over thirty different kinds of clouds but have separated them into three main types: cirrus, cumulus, and stratus.
2. Correct.
3. A recent Gallup poll found that Americans only consider one activity more stressful than visiting the dentist: hosting a dinner party.
4. Mr. and Mrs. Garden Slug loved their wedding gift: a set of salt and pepper shakers.
5. Please remember to buy the following at the pet store: one pound of cat food, two flea collars, kitty fang floss, a bag of catnip, and thirty-six lint rollers.
6. The Director of Academic Services at Pennsylvania State University once nominated this sentence for Outstanding Grammar Error of the Year: "I had to leave my good friend's behind and find new ones."
7. Some of the cars manufactured between 1907 and 1912 that didn't achieve the popularity of the Model T were the Black Crow, the Swallow, the Bugmobile, and the Carnation.
8. There's only one thing that can make our lawn look as good as our neighbor's: snow.
9. In a Thurmont, Maryland, cemetery can be found this epitaph: "Here lies an Atheist, all dressed up and no place to go."
10. George Bernard Shaw, the famous playwright, claimed he wanted the following epitaph on his tombstone: "I knew if I stayed around long enough, something like this would happen."

Errors with Apostrophes

Practicing What You've Learned, p. 585

A. 1. A horse's pajamas
   2. The queen's throne
   3. A family's vacation
   4. Ten students' grades
   5. The Depression of the 1930s was over.
   6. That dress of hers
   7. The children's toys
   8. Worms for sale
   9. Bill Jones' (or Jones's) car
   10. All essays are due today.
   11. Sign both the painter's and the roofer's contracts.
   12. Women's hats with feathers for decoration

B. 1. It's unfortunate that the game ended in a tie.
   2. The tree lost its leaves.
   3. It's beginning to feel like fall now.
   4. The library was closing its doors.
   5. I realize it's none of my business.

Assignment, p. 586

During winter parties there's often one ignored dessert on the buffet table: the fruitcake. If you're a fruitcake-hater on someone's annual holiday gift list, don't just throw it out—dump it in style! Attend the Great Fruitcake Toss in Manitou Springs, Colorado, a whacky series of contests held every first Saturday in January since 1996. Contestants vie for the longest throw, for the most accurate toss, and for the most creative launching device. In years past, hurlers have used catapults, cannons, slingshots, bows and arrows, and giant rubber-band contraptions to fling their fruitcakes; only eating is strictly forbidden. It's all done for charity; the entrance fee of one nonperishable food item for the town's food bank fills the shelves for weeks.

Errors with Apostrophes and Quotation Marks

Practicing What You've Learned, p. 588

1. It's true that when famous wit Dorothy Parker was told that President Coolidge, also known as "Silent Cal," was dead, she exclaimed, "How can they tell?"
2. When a woman seated next to Coolidge at a dinner party once told him she had made a bet with a friend that she could get more than two words out of him, he replied, "You lose."
3. Twenty-one of Elvis Presley's albums have sold over a million copies; twenty of The Beatles' albums have also done so.
4. Cinderella's stepmother wasn't pleased that her daughter received an "F" in her creative writing class on her poem "Seven Guys and a Gal," which she had plagiarized from her two friends Snow White and Dopey.
5. "Wasn't it Mae West who said, 'When choosing between two evils, I always like to try the one I've never tried before'?" asked Olivia.
6. Horace said, "Believe me, it's to everybody's advantage to sing the popular song 'You Stole My Heart and Stomped That Sucker Flat,' if that's what the holdup man wants."

98

7. A scholar's research has revealed that the five most commonly used words in written English are "the," "of," "and," "a," and "to." (Italicizing the words in quotation marks would also be correct.)
8. The triplets' mother said that while it's hard for her to choose, O. Henry's famous short story "The Ransom of Red Chief " is probably her favorite.
9. Despite both her lawyers' advice, she used the words "terrifying," "hideous," and "unforgettable" to describe her latest flight on Golden Fleece Airways, piloted by Jack "One-Eye" Marcus. (Italicizing "terrifying," "hideous," and "unforgettable" would also be correct.)
10. It's clear that Bubba didn't know if the Christmas tree thrown in the neighbors' yard was ours, theirs, or yours.

Errors with Parentheses, Brackets, and Dashes

Practicing What You've Learned, p. 592

1. Correct.
2. . . . [Editor's note: For help with apostrophes, see pages 509–510 in this text.]
3. . . . (sixteen pairs of twins, seven sets of triplets, and four sets of quadruplets).
4. . . . childrens [sic] . . . .
5. . . . his cards right—his Visa card, his Mastercard, his American Express card.

Errors with Hyphens

Practicing What You've Learned, p. 593

1. first-class event
2. well-done steak
3. self-employed person
4. Correct
5. one-word answer
6. Correct
7. once-in-a-lifetime experience
8. fifteen-year-old girl
9. overly excited
10. fifty-sixth birthday
11. Correct
12. The hard-boiled detective omitted an important detail in his report.

Errors with Italics and Underlining

Practicing What You've Learned, p. 595

1. page six of the *New York Times*
2. the popular novel *The Great Gatsby*
3. an article in *Time* magazine
4. watching the episode "The Puffy Shirt" on *Seinfeld*
5. movie stars in *The Dark Knight*
6. confusing the words *to*, *too*, and *two*
7. the first act of *Death of a Salesman*
8. remembering the words to "The Star-Spangled Banner"
9. the sinking of the *Edmund Fitzgerald*
10. missing my *abuela* in Texas

Errors with Parentheses, Brackets, Dashes, Hyphens, Italics, Ellipses, and Slashes

Practicing What You've Learned, p. 596

1. Many moviegoers know that the ape in *King Kong* (the original 1933 version, not the remake) was only an eighteen-inch-tall animated figure, but not everyone realizes that the Red Sea Moses parted in the 1923 movie of *The Ten Commandments* was a quivering slab of Jell-O sliced down the middle.

2. We recall the last words of General John B. Sedgwick at the Battle of Spotsylvania in 1864: "They couldn't hit an elephant at this dist...."

3. In a person-to-person telephone call, the twenty-five-year-old starlet promised the hardworking gossip columnist that she would "tell the truth and nothing but the truth" about her highly publicized feud with her ex-husband, editor-in-chief of *Meat-Eaters' Digest*.

4. While sailing across the Atlantic aboard the celebrity-filled yacht the *Titanic II*, Dottie Mae Haskell (she's the author of the popular new self-help book *Finding Wolves to Raise Your Children*) confided that until recently, she thought "chutzpa" [or *chutzpa*] was an Italian side dish. (Dashes instead of parentheses would be correct too.)

5. During their twenty-four-hour sit-in at the melt-down site, the anti-nuclear protesters began to sing, "Oh, say can you see...."

6. Few people know that James Arness (later Matt Dillon in the long-running television series *Gunsmoke*) got his start by playing the vegetable creature in the postwar monster movie *The Thing* (1951). (For more emphasis, substitute dashes for the parentheses.)

7. If you do not pay your rent on time, your landlord has the right to charge a late fee and/or begin an eviction procedure.

8. A French chemist named Georges Claude invented the first neon sign in 1910. (For additional information on his successful attempts to use seawater to generate electricity, see pp. 200–205.)

9. When Lucille Ball, star of *I Love Lucy*, became pregnant with her first child, the network executives decided that the word *expecting* could be used on the air to refer to her condition, but not the word *pregnant*. ("Expecting" and "pregnant" are also correct.)

10. In mystery stories, the detective often advises the police to *cherchez la femme*. [Editor's note: *Cherchez la femme* means "look for the woman" in French.]

Chapter 22
A Concise Guide to Mechanics, p. 599

■ Summary

Capitalization
Practicing What You've Learned

Abbreviations

Numbers
Practicing What You've Learned

Assignment

Collaborative Activity

Spelling

■ Answers to "Practicing What You've Learned" Exercises

Errors with Capitalization

Practicing What You've Learned, p. 601

A.
1. delicious Chinese food
2. Memorial Day memories
3. fiery Southwestern salsa
4. his latest novel, *A Prince at Work*
5. Bible study at the Baptist church
6. Count Dracula's castle in Transylvania
7. African-American heritage
8. a Dodge van driven across the Golden Gate Bridge
9. Sunday morning newspapers
10. the British daughter-in-law of Senator Snort

B. Answers will vary.

Errors in Capitalization, Abbreviations, and Numbers

Practicing What You've Learned, p. 603

1. Speaking to students at Gallaudet University, Marian Wright Edelman, founder and president of the Children's Defense Fund, noted that an American child is born into poverty every 30 seconds, is born to a teen mother every 60 seconds, is abused or neglected every 26 seconds, is arrested for a violent crime every 5 minutes, and is killed by a gun every 2 hours.

2. My sister, who lives in the East, was amazed to read studies by Thomas Radecki, M.D., showing that twelve-year-olds commit 300% more murders than did the same age group thirty years ago.

3. In 67 C.E. the Roman Emperor Nero entered the chariot race at the Olympic Games, and although he failed to finish the race, the judges unanimously declared him the winner.

4. According to John Alcock, a behavioral ecologist at Arizona State University, in the U.S.A. the chances of being poisoned by a snake are twenty times less than those of being hit by lightning and three hundred times less than the risk of being murdered by a fellow American.

5. The official Chinese News Agency, located in the city of Xinhua, estimates that there are ten million guitar players in their country today, an amazing number considering that the instrument was banned during the Cultural Revolution, which lasted ten years, from 1966 to 1976.

6. Two hundred thirty-one electoral votes were cast for James Monroe but only one for John Quincy Adams in the 1820 presidential race.

7. The British soldier T. E. Lawrence, better known as "Lawrence of Arabia," stood less than five feet, six inches tall.

8. Before my 10 A.M. English class, held in Wrigley Field every other Friday, except on New Year's Day, I eat three pieces of French pastry.

9. When a political opponent once called him "two-faced," President Lincoln retorted, "If I had another face, do you think I would wear this one?"

10. Alexander Graham Bell, inventor of the telephone, died in Nova Scotia on August 2, 1922; two days later, on the day of his burial, for one minute no telephone in North America was allowed to ring.

Assignment, p. 604

Answers will vary.

Part 5
Additional Readings

■ Part Five Summary, p. 607

Exposition

- Development by Example, Process Analysis, Comparison/Contrast, Definition, Division/Classification, Causal Analysis

Argumentation

Description

Narration

Essays for Further Analysis: Multiple Strategies and Styles

Literature

Special note: Many of the questions and answers provided here were written by Christi Conti, Colleen D. Schaeffer, Kimberly Miller, Anne Machin, Larry Bromley, and several other teachers who have contributed to this Instructor's Manual through a number of editions. The questions posed here are by no means exhaustive, but, rather, are intended only to suggest possible areas of discussion, depending upon a particular reading's use in the classroom.

–J.W.

Chapter 23
Exposition: Development by Example, p. 609

■ **"Darkness at Noon" by Harold Krents—p. 609**

Questions on Content, Structure, and Style

1. What is Krents's thesis? Is it clearly stated?
2. How does Krents support his claims?
3. Of the examples presented, which is most effective? Why?
4. Which of Krents's examples is least effective? Explain.
5. Are there any points raised by Krents that would be strengthened by additional illustrative examples? Explain.
6. What is Krents's purpose in writing this essay? Who is his intended audience?
7. Describe Krents's tone (e.g., "at which point even my saint-like disposition deserted me").
8. What does Krents mean when he writes in his opening paragraph that he sees himself only in "the image I create in the eye of the observer. To date it has not been narcissistic"? Contrast this paragraph with his conclusion. Do they address the same issue? Why or why not?
9. How is Krents's essay organized? Does it follow a logical, effective order?
10. This essay was originally published in 1976. Is it still relevant today? Have Krents's hopes for the future come to pass? Cite examples to support your answer.

Answers to Questions

1. Krents's thesis is not overtly stated; instead, his claim that people with disabilities are the victims of ignorance-based discrimination is implicit in the essay.
2. The author's claim is supported with several personal experiences.
3. Students might argue that the hospital example, because of its vivid detail and dialogue use, is the most effective.
4. The example of being "turned down by over forty law firms" is perhaps less effective than the others since it is presented in such general terms. Krents notes that this "will always remain one of the most disillusioning experiences" of his life, yet it is not described in detail.
5. Showing one of the law firm rejections in detail, using dialogue and the same level of specific sensory detail as he did in the hospital example, would make Krents's description of this experience more powerful for the reader.
6. Krents's purpose in writing this essay, originally published for a general audience in *The New York Times,* is to show readers how ignorance and misperceptions can lead to discrimination.
7. Krents uses a combination of humorous examples—to illustrate the ludicrous treatment of the disabled—and honest, straightforward statements of frustration and hope to drive his points home.
8. The opening paragraph indicates that as he is blind, Krents "sees" himself as others see him, and because of public misperceptions it is not an overly flattering image. His concluding paragraphs imply that these misperceptions do not have to exist. Just as the young girl, in the innocence of childhood, does not recognize the handicap, so too can the plant manager learn to look beyond physical disabilities.

9. Krents's essay is organized logically by example, moving from instances where he experiences discrimination to experiences illustrating his hope that this discrimination will end.

10. Student responses to this question will vary, but all should be supported by examples. With fully developed examples, answers to this question could serve as the basis for student essays.

Vocabulary

1. narcissistic (1)—characterized by excessive love of self
2. enunciating (2)—pronouncing
3. conversely (2)—reciprocally, contrarily
4. graphically (5)—powerfully
5. disposition (13)—temperament
6. cum laude (15)—with distinction

■ "Black Men and Public Space" by Brent Staples—p. 611

Questions on Content, Structure, and Style

1. What effect on the reader does Staples intend with his opening line?
2. Does Staples use primarily hypothetical or specific examples as support? Why does he make that choice for this particular essay?
3. In paragraphs 6 and 7, the author tells of his boyhood in Chester, Pennsylvania. Why does he include this information?
4. Is Staples's thesis statement implicit or explicit? Write a thesis statement for this essay in your own words.
5. Staples includes an example in paragraph 10 of another black male journalist who experienced a similar negative reaction. Why does Staples include this example in addition to his own?
6. What are some of the more vivid details the author used to develop his examples? What is the impact of those details on the reader?
7. This essay was written in 1986. Do you believe these same experiences could happen today? In your community?
8. What prejudices have you experienced or witnessed? Besides race, what other stereotypes are held today and are causing people to be prejudged? Are stereotypes always negative?
9. In paragraph 5, Staples says "young black males are overrepresented among the perpetrators of that violence [toward women]." What does he mean? Why does he acknowledge that fact?
10. What is the tone of this essay? What evidence can you cite to support your answer? Does the conclusive paragraph provide evidence that Staples has adequately learned to deal with the problem, or is there evidence of some residual bitterness in the conclusion?

Answers to Questions

1. Staples intends to shock the reader to attention with this overstated, purposeful misrepresentation of his experience.
2. The specific, real examples are important in this essay because, without them, a reader might accuse Staples of whining or misinterpreting people's actions. When he provides exact incidences, the reader can see how often Staples actually was prejudged and understand how frustrating those experiences must have been for him.
3. Knowing that Staples was a "good kid" and that, while he saw violence in his home town, he was not part of it, is important for the reader in order to understand why he was so surprised at the reactions he received. Also, he was "scarcely noticeable" in his hometown in contrast to the constant awareness and suspicion he experienced in Chicago and New York.

4. The complexity of Staples's thesis is not explicitly stated in the essay, although a very concise summary of the topic appears in paragraph 11: "Over the years, I learned to smother the rage I felt at so often being taken for a criminal." A more complete thesis statement would include a clearer indication of his attitude toward these experiences: "After many negative experiences of being stereotyped as a potential criminal, I have unfortunately had to change my appearance and behavior to avoid being perceived as threatening because of my race."

5. Showing that other black males have the same experiences indicates the problem is larger than just his own and that he has not imagined or exaggerated his situation.

6. Staples describes himself ("a broad six feet two inches with a beard and billowing hair, both hands shoved into the pockets of a bulky military jacket") so that the reader can imagine the vision that threatened his "victim." The "thunk, thunk, thunk" of the door locks is also easy to imagine. The jewelry store owner ("her eyes bulging nearly out of her head") and her "enormous red Doberman pinscher straining at the end of a leash" help the reader picture the fear people feel when he confronts them.

7. Student responses will vary.

8. Students can relate to Staples's experience more closely when they discuss the types of stereotyping in which they have been involved. Teenagers certainly are stereotyped and others have instant stock reactions to them in many cases. They might also discuss religious and gender prejudices they have experienced.

9. Students often misread this statement. They often think Staples is saying that blacks are incorrectly suspected of being violent while he is actually conceding that more blacks than whites *are*, in fact, perpetrators of violence against women—he's just not one of them. This concession is important to show the reader that he is attempting to be very fair about his observations.

10. Student opinions will differ very strongly on this question. Some will believe Staples is comfortable with the adjustment he has made while others will see an underlying edge to his resignation with the system. Staples's tone is not lividly angry, but he is unhappy that his race has to live with and accommodate such prejudice.

Vocabulary

1. unwieldy (2)—hard to manage
2. dicey (2)—questionable
3. errant (2)—wandering from a regular course
4. taut (4)—tight, tense
5. warrenlike (5)—as a crowded group of buildings
6. solace (5)—consolation, comfort
7. perilous (8)—dangerous
8. ad hoc (8)—for this case only
9. skittish (11)—easily frightened
10. congenial (11)—friendly, compatible

■ "Thank You" by Alex Haley—p. 613

Questions on Content, Structure, and Style

1. What is Haley's purpose for writing this essay?
2. Who are the living influences in Haley's life?
3. What examples does Haley provide to illustrate influence on his life?
4. How do Haley's examples convey a tone of sincerity to both the letters' recipients and the readers of Haley's essay?
5. How do Haley's loved ones react to his letters of thanksgiving?

6. What examples does Haley provide to demonstrate the continued effects of his first exercise in thanksgiving?
7. What is the significance of Haley's personal motto: "Find the good—and praise it?" How does this motto relate to the theme of this essay?
8. How is this essay similar in theme to that of "The Teacher Who Changed My Life," by Nicholas Gage, which appears in Chapter 28?

Answers to Questions

1. Haley spent the Thanksgiving of 1943 on a naval ship during World War II. After preparing a Thanksgiving feast for his fellow sailors, he spends the evening reflecting on the holiday and realizes that there are three people in his life to whom he owes thanks. These letters had great impact on their recipients' lives as well as Haley's own. He writes this essay to urge readers to similarly enrich the lives of people who have inspired or influenced their own lives.

2. Haley's living influences at the time were his father, Simon A. Haley, his grandmother, Cynthia Palmer, and his grammar school principal, Reverend Lonual Nelson.

3. Haley thanked his father for teaching him to love books. Haley recalls memories of discussing literature and vocabulary over the dinner table, and notes his father's influence on Haley's writing career. Ironically, in 1982, when this essay was written, long before the invention of YouTube, text messaging, or social networking sites, Haley mourns for a generation of children who are "so immersed in the electronic media that they have little to no awareness of the wondrous world to be discovered in books" (14). Haley then thanks Reverend Nelson for his morning prayers at school assemblies and acknowledges that those prayers have had great and meaningful influence on his life. Haley's grandmother is thanked for her instructions in morality, and Haley recalls her lessons in telling the truth, sharing, and forgiveness. He sweetly and sentimentally also thanks her for having "sprinkled [his] life with stardust" (16).

4. Haley's use of detailed examples shows that his letters are sincere. By thanking each person for what he or she has specifically done for Haley, he demonstrates that the person's influence has not been forgotten. The precise examples lend a note of authenticity to Haley's thanksgiving.

5. Haley's recipients are touched by his thanks and their responses leave Haley feeling "astounded" and "humbled." Each letter recipient provided Haley with examples of their own hopes, fears, and strengths and described the delight that Haley's expressions of gratitude had brought them.

6. Haley offers several more examples of thanksgiving's positive effects. He continues to thank those who impact his life, especially persons working in the service industry, and encourages students to thank their elders. Haley has also been on the receiving end of thanksgiving: in paragraph 26, he describes the joy he has personally gotten from receiving "thank you" letters from readers.

7. Haley's motto, "Find the good—and praise it," adequately sums up his grateful attitude. The motto encourager readers to recognize and appreciate the positives in their lives.

8. Gage follows Haley's advice, as his essay is a tribute to his teacher Miss Hurd for making such a significant contribution to his education and career. (Teachers may wish to pair these two essays in advance of an assignment asking students to remember and express gratitude to an important person in their lives.)

Vocabulary

1. indelibly (10)—making marks that cannot be erased
2. fo'c'sle (3 and 10)—a nautical term for shelter
3. nostalgia (16)—a wistful desire to return in thought or in fact to a former time in one's life
4. rendezvous (18)—an agreement between two or more persons to meet at a certain time and place
5. buoyant (27)—tending to float in a fluid

Chapter 24
Exposition: Process Analysis, p. 617

■ "The Jeaning of America" by Carin C. Quinn—p. 617

Questions on Content, Structure, and Style

1. Quinn maintains that jeans are a symbol of the American way of life. What do they symbolize?
2. What are the main stages or steps in this process analysis?
3. This essay follows the development of blue jeans to 1978, when it was written. What stages would you add to the process to bring it up to date?
4. What does the narrative of Strauss's life add to this process analysis?
5. What descriptive details add more interest to the process of the invention and development of blue jeans?
6. Why do you think Quinn has chosen this topic to research and write about? What is her audience and purpose?
7. Where do you see transitional devices used to tie pieces of the process together?
8. What strategy does Quinn use to develop the concluding paragraph?
9. Our American culture has been known as a "melting pot" of many other cultures, and everywhere we can find French, English, Spanish, and German influences, among various others. What other distinctly American institutions/practices/objects such as blue jeans can you think of ?
10. What objects that are an accepted part of your life might be interesting to trace back to their origins?

Answers to Questions

1. Blue jeans symbolize equality, ruggedness, frontier spirit and innovation.
   a. Strauss goes west with canvas because he cannot make a living with his brothers.
   b. Strauss encounters a miner who complains about wearing out his pants.
   c. Strauss makes the miner pants from his fabric and the miner is enthusiastic about them.
   d. Fabric is changed to serge de Nimes (denim) by accident.
   e. Rivets are added by Davis as a joke.
   f. Easterners discover jeans in the 1950s at dude ranches.
   g. Popularity explodes during WWII with factory workers.
   h. Jeans are made all over the world and sold in great numbers.
2. Students might mention that there are now a multitude of manufacturers, styles, and colors; that the jean "look" has come to jackets, skirts, shirts, and shorts; that they are never supposed to look new now, but stonewashed and worn; that a whole new fashion statement has developed with torn, frayed, patched, and bleach-spotted jeans; or that "vintage jeans" have become an international phenomenon.
3. Without Strauss's personal history, the analysis would be a dry listing of events and dates; his story humanizes the process. Students might be encouraged to personalize their essays with anecdotes when appropriate.
4. Descriptive details that enliven the process are specific names, particularly Alkalai Ike, hauling 180 pounds of goods door to door, the fabric names and derivation of the term "jeans," numbers of jeans sold, and many others.

5. Quinn could be sure, when she picked this topic, that a broad readership would take blue jeans for granted and might be intrigued by the interesting and quirky process by which they were created and developed. Her purpose is probably both informative and entertaining.

6. Since the essay is arranged temporally, transitions related to time are used throughout: for two years, when, by this time, each year, etc.

7. The conclusion is a paragraph developed by example.

8. There are many possibilities for response, such as barbecuing, rodeo, hot dogs, and football.

9. Students will find many objects they take for granted but seldom do they know how the object came to exist: skis, sunglasses, CDs, computers, neckties, Stetsons or ball caps, pieces of sports equipment (e.g., the refinement of baseball bats), etc.

Vocabulary

1. ubiquitous (2)—seeming to be present everywhere
2. emigrated (3)—departed from a place or country
3. eke (3)—manage to make a living (or find a solution) with difficulty
4. beckoned (4)—called or summoned by a slight gesture
5. pacify (5)—to calm, make peaceful
6. prospered (6)—thrived, flourished
7. commodity (6)—an article bought or sold
8. proletarian (6)—working class
9. idiosyncratic (6)—having a peculiar personal mannerism

■ "I Slalomly Swear" by Dave Barry—p. 619

Special note: Teachers who used the previous edition of this text may recognize Barry's essay under a different title; at Barry's request, the title "I Slalomly Swear" replaces "Skiing Lessons: The Cold, Hard Facts."

Questions on Content, Structure, and Style

1. Is Barry's introduction effective? How so?
2. Who is Barry's audience? What indicates this to you?
3. Does Barry's advice cover all the "steps" required to learn how to ski? Why or why not?
4. What organizational devices/strategies does Barry use?
5. What is Barry's tone in paragraph 2? Can you find other instances of its use?
6. What is the effect of putting "hit the slopes" in quotation marks? Look at Barry's uses of quotation marks elsewhere in the text. Do the marks contribute anything to the author's meaning beyond the expected?
7. How does Barry's style and title reflect the purpose and tone of his content?
8. Is this a directional or informative process?

Answers to Questions

1. Barry begins with a direct statement about family vacations and moves the reader immediately into his topic. He does so with a sense of humor, thus preparing us for what is to follow. He does not exactly reveal that he will be discussing the steps to skiing in the introduction, but he has given us a preview into the fact that he is not a skilled skier in the statement "potentially knocking down a tree with your face." Since Barry's humoristic style is of a type, he clues the reader into it immediately and thus provides us with an opening that allows us to relax at his expense.

2. Barry begins by addressing vacation seekers who might be interested in a family ski trip, but his essay can be enjoyed by anyone.

3. No. He generally discusses the costs, financial and physical, which are the main purposes of his essay.

4. Barry begins with planning and then moves to the ski lessons. But he proceeds through each in a series of steps related to each. Within this construct he also uses cause and effect—a "special outfit" will cost you plenty and make you look like a "Giant Radioactive Easter Bunny From Space," goggles will fog up and will potentially cause you to crash into a tree, boots will cut off your blood circulation, etc.

5. Barry's tone is sarcastic. Responses will vary.

6. Barry's use of quotation marks might first be observed as simply identifying a cliché. However, when the entire context of the dangers of skiing are brought to bear, his use can be seen as a matter of highlighting an unpleasant aspect of skiing. The statement "hit the slopes" echoes "knocking down a tree with your face." Likewise, "Gore-Tex" has a similar ring. Other uses highlight Barry's sarcasm.

7. Barry's style is to use sarcasm to make us laugh at social constructs and expectations. The lesson learned here is that skiing is an absurd activity that may be more entertaining and less costly to watch than to experience. "Slalomly" is a play on words: "slalom" (ski on a zigzag course) for "solemn" (earnest).

8. This is a tongue-in-cheek directional process essay, with Barry taking humorous liberties in his "how to take a ski vacation" advice.

■ "Successful Presentations: Some Practical Advice" by Margaret McDonald—p. 621

Questions on Content, Structure, and Style

1. What is the purpose of the opening two paragraphs?
2. Who is McDonald's target audience?
3. Is McDonald's essay an informative or directional process essay?
4. What steps does McDonald suggest for readers who want to improve their presentation skills?
5. How does McDonald move the reader from one point to another in her advice?
6. Notice McDonald's sentence structure. What is the purpose of using such simple, short sentences?
7. How do McDonald's tone and diction contribute to her essay?
8. Examine the final paragraph. Does it conclude the essay effectively? Why or why not?

Answers to Questions

1. The opening paragraphs describe a common experience to which most readers can relate: the discomfort of having to listen to a poorly executed presentation. McDonald then offers some suggestions for successful speech-making.

2. McDonald is writing for people who need help refining their speaking skills.

3. McDonald's essay is a directional process essay. She explains how to avoid a weak presentation.

4. First, McDonald advises readers to speak slowly and pause when giving presentations. Next, readers are advised to stay on topic and not contradict themselves. Good speakers and presenters are also organized. Good speakers also avoid "ums," "ahs," and "verbal tics." Readers are also advised to have a clear conclusion and a limited amount of question and answer time after the presentation. Finally, speakers are advised to thank their audience for their attention.

110

5. Because this is a newspaper article and space is at a premium, McDonald uses a series of bulleted paragraphs instead of offering paragraphs linked with a variety of transitional words and/or phrases. Students might discuss times when such a list might be appropriate in their own writing.
6. McDonald writes as if she were going to deliver it orally. She uses simple, short sentences that are easy for readers to process the information.
7. McDonald's casual, informative tone and her clear, concise diction provide a strong example for readers hoping to improve their communication skills. She advises readers to stay on topic, to organize their presentations, and to have a clear conclusion, and she models these steps in her essay.
8. The final paragraph demonstrates her advice for closing a presentation. Students might practice writing a more emphatic conclusion.

Vocabulary

1. toilsome (1)—laborious or fatiguing
2. ethnographic (3))—adjective form of ethnography, the scientific description of specific human cultures
3. droning (5)—talking in a boring voice

Chapter 25
Exposition: Comparison/Contrast, p. 623

■ **"My Real Car" by Bailey White—p. 623**

Questions on Content, Structure, and Style

1. In order to be worth a reader's time, a comparison/contrast essay must have a point—a reason for looking at similarities and differences. Why does White compare these two vehicles?
2. Why does White spend much more time describing her "real" car than the new one?
3. A good comparison/contrast discusses parallel points about "Subject A" and "Subject B." What are the points White examines relative to the two cars?
4. To what senses does White appeal in her description of the two vehicles?
5. Much of what White tells the reader about her "real" car involves inconvenience. Where do you see glimpses of her affection for the car, despite its problems?
6. After reading about the new car, what do you think Bailey White's attitude is toward it?
7. What encounters with cars like the "real" car have you had on the road? What new perspective on those encounters might this essay give you?
8. Evaluate White's conclusion.
9. If you took White for a ride in your car, or your family car, what observations might she—and you—make about it?
10. What object have you replaced that had sentimental value? Why was the replacement either a satisfaction or a disappointment for you?

Answers to Questions

1. White believes there is a certain emotional and sentimental value in possessions that cannot be equaled or replaced by a newer substitute.
2. The value and long-term connection with which White regards the old car is more important to her than the rather emotionless and sterile quality of the new car.
3. White compares exterior appearance, starting procedure, interior and comfort, sound, and ride ("We floated down the road").
4. White appeals to four of the senses: sight, touch, hearing, smell.
5. As well as several other places, White's last paragraph shows her connection to the car, which she still enjoys; paragraph 8, "a little smell of me," also demonstrates her bond with the car.
6. White appears to appreciate the convenience and comfort of the new car, but doesn't have the affection for it that she will always have for the other automobile, which is full of memories.
7. Students' answers will vary; many may comment that they now understand there may be an interesting and clever person behind the wheel and that their stereotypes may be far from reality.
8. The concluding line supports White's view of her "real car," though some readers may find the essay's ending slightly abrupt.
9. Student responses will vary.
10. Student responses will vary.

Vocabulary

1. odometer (5)—a mileage gauge
2. ominous (9)—threatening, sinister, menacing

■ "The Myth of the Latin Woman: I Just Met a Girl Named Maria" by Judith Ortiz Cofer—p. 625

Questions on Content, Structure, and Style

1. The passage opens with a reference to "Maria" from *West Side Story*. What is the significance of this scene? What do the young man's actions imply?
2. What is Cofer's purpose for writing?
3. What stereotypes do the terms "Hot Tamale" and "sexual firebrand" suggest about Latina women? What stereotypes appear later in the essay? How do these stereotypes affect Cofer?
4. What challenges does Cofer face as a young girl attempting to assimilate into mainstream American culture?
5. In addition to comparing styles of dress, what other cultural comparisons does Cofer make?
6. Discuss Latin family values. How do these compare and contrast with mainstream American family values?
7. In paragraph 9, a teenaged Cofer compares herself to fruit or vegetable: "I was supposed to *ripen*, not just grow into womanhood like other girls." What is the significance of this statement and how does it contribute to the overall effect of the essay?
8. Now that Cofer is an adult, does the mainstream public view her differently, or do the stereotypes from her youth continue to affect her?
9. How does Cofer use her poetry as a catalyst for change?
10. What other cultural groups continue to be marginalized by mainstream society?

Answers to Questions

1. *West Side Story*, a Broadway musical based on William Shakespeare's *Romeo and Juliet*, focuses on two rival gangs, a group of young Puerto Ricans and a group of young Caucasians. One of the white boys falls for Maria, the sister of the Puerto Rican gang's leader. The London scene at the beginning of Cofer's essay is significant because it is an example of gross stereotyping. The young British man sees a Hispanic woman, assumes she is like the character in the play, and begins serenading Cofer. This type of stereotyping connects to the title of Cofer's work: "I just met a girl named Maria" is a line from the song "Maria" in *West Side Story* and the myth Cofer refers to is that all Latina women are the same.
2. Cofer wants to educate readers about her culture and discourage unfair stereotypes.
3. Terms such as "Hot Tamale" and "sexual firebrand" imply that Latinas are simply sexual beings. Other stereotypes Cofer addresses are the Latina as a domestic or criminal. These stereotypes infuriate and frustrate Cofer, and she states that her goal is to "replace the old pervasive stereotypes and myths about Latinas with a much more interesting set of realities" (4).
4. Cofer feels she has no guidance on how to dress or behave in order to assimilate with mainstream culture. There are no Latina role models in mainstream culture; in fact, the only Hispanic on television during Cofer's youth was a man.
5. She compares mainstream American parties to Puerto Rican parties and finds the American parties falling short in comparison. She also compares the way mainstream Americans see Puerto Ricans and the way Puerto Ricans identify themselves.
6. Cofer explains that in Puerto Rico, "women felt freer to dress and move more provocatively, since, in most cases, they were protected by the traditions, mores, and laws of a Spanish/Catholic

113

system of morality and machismo." The Puerto Rican culture advocated a system of "look, but don't touch," and if a woman was wronged, "everyone would close in to save her family honor." Student responses on their own family values will differ. Students may note differences in family values resulting from varying religious beliefs, cultures, and politics.

7. This statement is about Cofer's budding sexuality; because she was Latina, her date expected her to quickly develop into a sexual being. The example supports Cofer's argument that Latinas are unfairly stereotyped.

8. Cofer is still haunted by stereotypes and describes her experience of being mistaken for a waitress at her own book signing as an example of recent prejudice.

9. Cofer states, "Every time I give a reading, I hope the stories I tell, the dreams and fears I examine in my work, can achieve some universal truth which will get my audience past the particulars of my skin color, my accent, or my clothes" (14).

10. Answers will vary. Students may discuss a variety of racial, ethnic, economic, or other groups who are continue to face prejudice in our society.

Vocabulary

1. covet (1)—to wish for, especially eagerly
2. bodega (3)—a grocery store or wine shop
3. coalesce (5)—to grow together; to blend together
4. innuendo (7)—an indirect intimation about or person or thing, especially of a derogatory nature
5. chromosomes (8)—any of several threadlike bodies that carry genes in a linear order
6. provocatively (8)—tending to provoke; inciting, stimulating
7. machismo (8)—a strong or exaggerated sense of manliness; an exaggerated sense of the right to dominate
8. promenade (9)—a stroll or walk, especially in a public place, as for pleasure or display
9. ditty (10)—a short, simple song
10. regale (10)—to entertain lavishly or agreeably

■ "Once More to the Lake (August 1941)" by E.B. White—p. 629

Questions on Content, Structure, and Style

What contrasts are set up in the first paragraph? What language suggests this?
1. White uses several extended metaphors in this essay. What comparisons are made in paragraph 2?
2. What is the dominant impression in this essay?
3. Identify a few particularly strong images that contribute to the dominant impression.
4. Why does the narrator return to the lake? What does he expect to get from the trip?
5. While White's essay is primarily organized through comparison, what additional organizational strategies does he employ?
6. The narrator repeats the words *peace, goodness,* and *jollity* in paragraph 10, which he had previously used in paragraph 9. These keywords tie into the overall theme but because the word order shifts from one paragraph to the other, there seems to be a shifting in the theme as well. What other statements indicate that not all is as it once was?
7. Other than a nostalgic, descriptive narrative, what is White's purpose?
8. Why is the date (August 1941) in the title significant?
9. Paragraph 12 relates the events of a summer thunderstorm. If viewed as a metaphor, what possible meanings can be found in this passage that would lend greater meaning to the final sentence?

Answers to Questions

1. White contrasts noise and quiet, stress and relaxation, and the moods associated with times and places. Keywords that suggest these contrasts are found in the harsh descriptions of the ocean—"restlessness of the tides," "fearful cold of the sea water," and "incessant wind"—versus the soft qualities of the lake itself and the first memories he relates—"the placidity of the lake," "kittens," "Pond's Extract" (a bit of a pun), and even "ringworm," which, although not a pleasant thought, does have a certain edgeless feeling about it.

2. White compares the lake and the woods that surround it to a cathedral. More than that, however, is a comparison between the holiness of the place and family, for it is in the memory that he recalls the stillness and the respect not to disturb it or his family.

3. The dominant impression is one of a tranquil connection between the past and present.

4. Responses will vary but the majority of them ought to come from the five senses—"I felt the same damp moss . . . saw the dragonfly alight . . ." (5); "the first smell of the pine laden air . . . no fuss, no loud wonderful fuss" (9).

5. The narrator returns presumably to relax, but there is an underlying element in his associations that clearly causes him to remember his father and so he may also be trying to determine what kind of relationship his father built with him. This aspect of the text is somewhat vague, however, and there is more emphasis on episodic scenes wherein memories intertwining with the present produce a focus on tranquil continuity.

6. Chronology primarily, which he uses to return the reader's orientation back to the present, is also interspersed with spatial description and descriptive episodes of memory.

7. Students will have many options here, but a few clearly indicate shifts in focus: "There had always been three tracks to choose from . . . ; now the choice was narrowed down to two" (7); "The waitresses were still fifteen; their hair had been washed, that was the only difference" (7); "The postcards that showed things looking a little better than they looked" (8), etc.

8. Again, responses will vary, but the strongest theme seems to be one of family and connections through time, the passing along of traditions both through the narrator and the narration itself. In paragraph 12 he notes a "joke about getting drenched linking the generations in a strong indestructible chain" and thus clues the reader to the cultural connections people share when they share experiences. He attempts to bridge time and place by keying into rural life and the idyllic. The story has a pastoral quality that establishes a mood of reflection early on and then sustains it till the very last line, which abruptly shifts the tone toward fear.

9. The year 1941 is significant in that it is the year the United States officially entered World War II. It also marked the establishment of the Atlantic Charter, a document that linked the United States and Great Britain as having in common certain principles in their respective national policies. It also became the year of the great push toward hydroelectric power, which may not at first seem significant, but could be considered relevant if one views this tale through a historical lens. The United States had been providing goods and producing war materials for those countries already engaged in the war. Sustaining such massive production required great quantities of power, and a good many dams were built for this purpose. While White makes no mention of his memorable lake as a source of power, he does very clearly suggest a connection to technological progress in paragraph 10 with the noise and the prevalence of "outboard" motors. There are multiple other connotations in paragraph 10 relating to boys learning to control motors, which surely provide additional areas for discussion and which also add to the layers of meaning White so deftly weaves. In terms of historical significance, however, the title provides an avenue of discussion for viewing America, and perhaps the world, in those prewar days as though through "a dropped curtain" (7), as representing youthful innocence and idealism and idyllic splendor. Published in 1941, White's text is a piece of Americana, whether he intended it to be or not.

10. Paragraph 12 relates the events of a summer thunderstorm and in doing so suggests a multitude of meanings. The general stereotypical associations involve change, impending doom, death, rebirth, cycles, etc. White's treatment of it is such that it at first appears to be one more episode that harkens to the past and sustains tradition. As such it can simply be viewed as a change in the weather that adds to the connections of human existence. Yet, it is a key aspect that the storm occurs near the end of the tale and seems to become a precursor to the final statement: "suddenly my groin felt the chill of death" (12). Responses will vary and should be encouraged through a writing assignment that allows them to explore more fully the richness of this essay.

Vocabulary

1. incessant (1)—nonstop
2. spinner (1)—a fishing lure
3. coves (2)—small secluded inlets or bays
4. tentatively (3)—subject to change or withdrawal
5. pensively (5)—thoughtfully
6. premonitory (12)—giving previous warning

Chapter 26
Exposition: Definition, p. 635

■ **"Celebrating Nerdiness" by Tom Rogers—p. 635**

Questions on Content, Structure, and Style

1. How does Rogers initially define a nerd?
2. Why does Rogers begin with the definition he does?
3. Who is the author's audience? How do you know?
4. What is the author's purpose? How can you tell?
5. How does Rogers want nerds to be viewed? (How does he redefine?)
6. What strategy does the author use in paragraph 3 to transition between the stereotypical definition and his own?
7. Identify some other strategies of definition that Rogers uses in his essay.
8. The tone in the essay shifts perceptibly throughout the essay. Compare a few paragraphs. Where is Rogers sarcastic? Humorous? Fatherly? Defensive? Can you find others?
9. Where is Rogers's thesis? Does its placement seem appropriate? Why?
10. In paragraphs 4 through 10, Rogers links his discussion and his paragraphs through an ongoing discussion of his children. How does he link paragraph 1 to paragraph 2? 2 to 3? 3 to 4?

Answers to Questions

1. Initially, Rogers uses the stereotype: "friendless, book-smart sissies who suck up to authority figures."
2. He provides a recognizable characterization to invite the reader in to compare and contrast the simplistic view with a personal one.
3. The author is writing both to other nerds and to the public. In general, he chooses to include himself in the category of nerd and identifies himself as a teacher, thus alerting the audience to his personal perspective and, perhaps, an intent to teach. But he uses the pronouns "we," "us," and "our," which allows readers to identify and benefit from his celebration.
4. The author's purpose is to celebrate nerds. The title gives it away. However, he has the additional purpose of negating a negative stereotype in the process, thereby disempowering it and empowering those who have been labeled nerds.
5. He redefines nerds through a comparison to famous inventors considered geniuses and then relates the success of his own children, showing them to be courageous in the face of social rejection and bullying, well-traveled, and witty.
6. Rogers transitions between the stereotype and his own definition in paragraph 3 by comparing and contrasting—nerds, in the abstract, famous nerd geniuses, nerds known personally. The personal representation allows for sympathetic response not found in the stereotype.
7. Other strategies found involve a description of characteristics (1); definition by negation—not "suck-ups" (1); compares to geniuses (3); gives examples (2, 5, 6, 8, 9, 10); discusses causes and effects (throughout); identifies times and places of use (1, 2, 3, 4, 10); and associates the term with recognizable people throughout but perhaps most notably in paragraph 3 and whenever he mentions school and bullies.
8. Answers will vary.

9. The thesis is the last sentence. It is appropriate here as Rogers invites the reader to participate in reformulating his/her own view to his idea without his having to defend it.

10. In paragraph one, he introduces himself as a nerd; in paragraph two he shifts from awareness of the label to a recollection of when he came to understand the effect of the label. In paragraph three, he explains how one effect caused another—his becoming a teacher—and then discusses how teachers partake, like others, in rejecting nerdiness despite the fact that such behavior is antithetical to their purpose. He then moves from the geniuses as examples to equating them to teens in American high schools, which then allows him to discuss his children in paragraph four and the remainder of the essay.

Vocabulary

1. inane (1)—insignificant
2. virtually (3)—almost; not real
3. eccentric (3)—odd, deviant from the norm
4. arrogant (3)—having a feeling of superiority and showing it to others
5. transcribed (8)—to make a copy of through writing

■ "The Picture of Health" by Kim Lute—p. 637

Questions on Content, Structure, and Style

1. How does Lute define "healthy"?
2. Who is Lute's audience?
3. How does Lute capture the reader's attention?
4. How do strangers define Lute (see paragraph 6)?
5. Lute describes herself as "fit, hard fought and hard won" (5). How does this phrase contribute to the tone of Lute's essay?
6. When does Lute's optimism wane?
7. In paragraph 9, Lute acknowledges that some people will continue to "punctuate every inquiry with condolences." What is meant by this statement and what is Lute's reaction?
8. How does your definition of "healthy" compare/contrast with Lute's?

Answers to Questions

1. Lute offers many definitions of healthy: "the absence of illness, frailties, and failings," "someone who's in constant pursuit of [health]" (5), but she also considers herself, someone who has suffered and overcome disease, "the picture of health" (3). In her conclusion, Lute explains that "any such definition [of healthy] will underscore that the presence of illness isn't nearly as important as one's ability to overcome it" (9).
2. Lute's essay was originally published in *Newsweek*, which suggests that she was writing for a wide, diverse audience. Anyone whose life has been touched by illness or anyone who values his or her health may find this essay interesting and thought-provoking.
3. The intimate descriptions of emotionally and physically painful procedures capture the audience's attention.
4. Strangers and some health care professionals view Lute differently than the way she sees herself. To some people, she is defined by her illnesses, her weaknesses, and her scars.
5. The phrase "fit, hard fought and hard won" exemplifies Lute's victorious, confident, and inspirational tone.
6. Lute's optimism occasionally wanes during a particularly painful or embarrassing medical procedure, but is restored when she considers all she has overcome.

118

7. Condolences, or words of sympathy, are implied by many people Lute encounters. She feels this sorrow or pity is unnecessary because she does not feel sorry for herself.
8. Responses will vary; students may define "healthy" in terms of physical or mental well-being.

Vocabulary

1. valet (4)—personal attendant
2. biopsy (4)—the removal of a sample of tissue from the body for examination
3. radiology (6)—a specialty of medicine that deals with the study and application of imaging technology such as x-ray and radiation to diagnose and treat disease
4. pathology (6)—the study and diagnosis of disease through examination of tissues, organs, and bodily fluids
5. wan (6)—sickly; pallid; lacking color
6. catheter (6)—a tube that can be inserted into a body cavity, duct, or vessel

■ "What Is Poverty?" by Jo Goodwin Parker—p. 638

Questions on Content, Structure, and Style

1. Summarize, as concisely as possible, Parker's definition of poverty.
2. What techniques does the author use to develop her definition? Note those that are especially effective.
3. Note the structure of the essay, with many paragraphs beginning "Poverty is . . .". Why is this effective?
4. What is Parker's purpose? Describe her intended audience (referred to as "you" in the essay; see paragraph 12).
5. As the biographical sketch of Parker at the beginning of the essay notes, little is known about her, including whether she is, in fact, writing from personal experience or whether she is an observer, using first-person point of view for effect. Does her identity matter to you as a reader, affecting the impact of the essay? Explain.
6. Is Parker aware of people who would be unsympathetic to her claims? If so, how does she address these people and their beliefs in the essay?
7. What parts of Parker's definition would be strengthened by additional development? Explain.
8. Parker relies on personal (subjective) experience to present her definition. Is this sufficient to convince her readers? Explain.
9. Characterize Parker's tone. She asks the reader to "listen without pity," yet does her tone evoke pity, or is it her subject that raises pity in the audience?
10. Compare Parker's opening and closing paragraphs. What emotional effect does she hope to have on her audience?

Answers to Questions

1. Parker defines poverty by powerfully describing how the poor must live—an existence of deprivation, illness, filth, fear, shame, and despair.
2. Parker employs a wrenching first-person narrative style that refers directly to the reader ("you") to describe and define poverty. She offers extensive, blunt personal illustrations of the daily life of the desperately poor, a stark contrast to the lives of most of her readers.
3. This repeated phrase jolts the reader with its relentlessness: over and over the phrase introduces a new horror to the reader, just as the poor must face ceaseless devastation.

4. Parker's purpose is to graphically reveal the true nature of poverty rather than offer a sanitized sociological definition. Her intended audience is those who have never known poverty and perhaps blame the poor for their condition.
5. Student responses to this question will vary; positions should be well explained.
6. Parker directly addresses individuals who are unsympathetic to the poor. Examples include paragraph 4 where she responds to the statement "Anybody can be clean." In paragraph 11 she notes, "But you say to me, there are schools." In both cases Parker answers the beliefs of these critics with her own experience.
7. Among the points that students might indicate need further development are those raised in paragraph 10 (children isolated from their peers by poverty; how poverty tempts children toward crime, drugs, and alcohol). Additional development might underscore the cyclical nature of poverty that Parker implies.
8. Parker does not pretend to offer anything more than her own experience to her readers so this narrative emerges as a powerful personal statement. While the addition of outside evidence would broaden Parker's base of support, it might also diminish the raw strength of the essay.
9. While readers may find that they do feel pity for the situation Parker describes, the description itself is not maudlin or filled with pathos. Instead, it is brutally direct and unflinching.
10. The opening and closing paragraphs of the essay highlight Parker's desire to move her reader to anger and action rather than passive sympathy.

Vocabulary

1. privy (2)—latrine, outhouse
2. chronic (3)—of a long duration or frequent recurrence
3. oleo (4)—margarine
4. pinkeye (11)—highly contagious eye infection

Chapter 27
Exposition: Division/Classification, p. 643

■ "Party Manners" by Richard L. Grossman—p. 643

Questions on Content, Structure, and Style

1. Is this an essay developed by classification or division?
2. What is Grossman's thesis in this essay?
3. What reaction do you think Grossman wants from his readers?
4. Are Grossman's categories distinct or are they overlapping and ambiguous?
5. Is there a natural order to these categories? Why might the author have picked this order of presentation?
6. As you read, you probably thought of people you know and specific experiences you have had. What could Grossman have done to make his categories even easier to picture?
7. The author is a medical professional. Does it surprise you that the director of a New York medical center would write like this? Grossman's tone and style in this essay are undoubtedly different from the writing voice he would use for an article for a medical journal. What does this tell you about his writing ability?
8. How does Grossman conclude his essay? Is this ending appropriate for his audience?

Answers to Questions

1. This essay classifies those kinds of party-goers who, in Grossman's opinion, are unveiling unresolved attitudes and hidden parts of their personalities that they would not show elsewhere.
2. Many people use a party as a medium for acting out their deficiencies or unresolved problems.
3. Students will have different ideas. Grossman probably wants readers to identify with their party experiences and see these types as legitimate, but he may also want readers to reflect on their own behavior and try to enjoy the "warmth and closeness of other human beings" (9) instead of acting out.
4. Yes, the categories are quite distinct.
5. No strong natural order is evident, but Grossman may have picked the more neurotic types for the end in order to build up more clearly to his conclusion.
6. Students will give examples from their own experience; examples would enliven and validate Grossman's categories.
7. Competent writers are flexible; they can adjust their style, language, and tone to the purpose and audience they are addressing.
8. Grossman directly addresses the reader, calling for self-examination of his or her own behavior at parties. As a medical professional, Grossman advocates therapy for those who might profit from it. This conclusion is appropriate for the readers of *Health* magazine, who are presumably interested in issues of mental, as well as physical, well-being.

Vocabulary

1. promenades (1)—public places for walking
2. ubiquitous (2)—seeming to be present everywhere

3. foibles (3)—small moral weaknesses
4. martyred (6)—having chosen to suffer
5. rueful (6)—causing sorrow or pity
6. haranguing (7)—giving a long, blustering, and pompous speech
7. cryptic (8)—having a hidden meaning

■ "The Extendable Fork" by Calvin Trillin—p. 646

Questions on Content, Structure, and Style

1. Does this essay illustrate primarily classification or division?
2. What is being classified, and what is Trillin's purpose?
3. What four types does Trillin describe?
4. How would you describe the tone of this essay? When were you first aware of this tone?
5. Why does Trillin begin his essay with reference to a new invention?
6. What is the effect of dialogue in this essay?
7. What does figurative language contribute to the descriptions in this essay?
8. Why does Trillin include comments about his own style of eating?
9. Evaluate Trillin's conclusion. How does it bring the essay full circle?
10. Are all of Trillin's categories equally developed? Does this present a problem for his readers?

Answers to Questions

1. Classification
2. Trillin classifies four kinds of long-reach eaters, those people who steal food off others' plates. Trillin's primary purpose is entertainment, but his comments should also make his readers think about their own eating habits (or nod in agreement recognizing people they know.)
3. The four types are The Finisher, The Waif, The Researcher, and the Simple Thief.
4. Trillin's essay is humorous; the names of the categories may tip off most readers that this is a lighthearted rather than serious classification essay.
5. The description of the extendable fork allows Trillin to launch into his classification of the long-reach eaters, as such folks (including the self-confessed Trillin himself) might profit from using this invention.
6. Dialogue shows some of the typical language used by the four types and thus makes Trillin's descriptions of them clearer (and also funnier.)
7. Again, the figurative language "like an urchin who has his nose pressed up against the window," "chicken…staked out on an anthill," "as quick as the strike of an adder" adds vividness and humor to Trillin's descriptions.
8. By incorporating personal examples Trillin exposes himself one of the "guilty" long-reach eaters, which keeps readers from seeing Trillin as merely critical of others.
9. Trillin returns to the new extendable fork, suggesting ways it and other inventions might "help" long-reach eaters achieve their dining goals.
10. No, they are not; the category of the Researcher, for instance, receives only a one-sentence description. Readers should understand that Trillin's classification is humorous, not a serious, in-depth treatment of a subject.

Vocabulary

1. urchin (4)—a mischievous boy
2. subterfuge (6)—a deception made strategic and used to save face or avoid detection
3. adder (8)—a type of snake

122

■ "Mother Tongue" by Amy Tan—p. 647

Questions on Content, Structure, and Style

1. One of Tan's purposes in this essay could be regarded as a search for her authentic voice. Do you think she finds it? If so, how does she define it?
2. Tan's discussion of speaking several Englishes might be recognizable to you if you've grown up speaking more than one language or using mixed languages such as Spanglish. Can you relate to her struggle in other ways that may be more universal?
3. Who is Tan's audience? How can you tell?
4. To clarify the different kinds of Englishes, what method of development does Tan frequently use?
5. What contributing factors led to Tan's desire to write this essay? What was her primary reason?
6. What does Tan note in paragraph 2 that influenced her to be a writer?
7. Speculate on influences other than those noted in paragraph 2 that may have caused her to become a writer.
8. How does paragraph 17 contribute to your understanding of why she chose to write rather than enter a profession in a math-related field, as she was encouraged to do?
9. While linguists might describe language in terms of sound, pronunciation, order, and meaning and grammarians in terms of rules and usage, how does language function for Tan? What does she examine?
10. In paragraph 20, Tan relates a line of text she omitted from her novel *The Joy Luck Club*. Why did she choose to omit it?

Answers to Questions

1. She finds it in her mother's speech, which she claims as her own when she names it as her mother tongue—the one she knows intimately and unconsciously, but becomes aware of only when she reflects on her mother's response to her book. She defines it as "vivid, direct, full of observation, and imagery"(7).
2. Students should be able to relate in terms of dialects they use with their friends versus those used at work or in the home or even with strangers. They may want to discuss how speech patterns differ and what patterns impart to the listener about self.
3. Tan is writing to those who have asked her questions about her writing, but her reflection is learned, even though she declares it mere opinion. It is considered and thoughtful and speaks to issues of language and language learning, so that she is most likely addressing both writers and students of writing as well as her colleagues and those curious about her as a curiosity—a successful Asian-American writer (18).
4. Tan often presents examples drawn from her mother's life and from her own experience.
5. Being asked to give a speech about her writing (3), having her mother in the audience and realizing she was using a kind of English she had never used with her mother (3), realizing that speech with her mother is habitual, familiar, and unnoticed as such on a day-to-day basis (4), understanding that people wrongly believe that those who speak imperfectly are somehow "broken" or less intellectually capable (7, 8), discovering the serious consequences or effects of such misperceptions when her mother could not get needed information from medical personnel (14), her own struggles with writing and tests in school (15–17), and finally because she was asked "why there are not more Asian Americans represented in American Literature. Why are there few Asian Americans enrolled in creative writing programs? Why do so many Chinese students go into engineering?" all contribute to her desire to write this essay. The latter set of questions would seem to be her primary reason for writing, so that this essay becomes her examination of causes and effect in an attempt to answer those questions.

6. She loves language, is "fascinated by language in daily life," spends time thinking about its "power" to "evoke an emotion, a visual image, a complex idea, or a simple truth" (2).

7. Responses will vary, but a primary influence most certainly must have been the fact that she spent most of her young life speaking for her mother, translating meaning for others, using a variety of Englishes in order to make meaning.

8. In paragraph 17, Tan relays that her primary mode of thought is not mathematical or orderly when she provides the example of word analogies. She emphasizes the fact that imagery has a more powerful hold on her thought and that to translate the problems into something meaningful she would need to create a mini-narrative, which she describes as an act of imagining an "associative situation."

9. Tan examines feelings and ideas. Language, for her, is the elemental tool for tapping into the heart of people and situations. In paragraph 21 she writes, "I wanted to capture what language ability tests can never reveal: her intent, her passion, her imagery, the rhythms of her speech and the nature of her thoughts."

10. Answers may vary. She omits it mainly because it is not authentic. It stifles, does not come naturally from her mouth or her mind. It is studied, and while the academic in her comprehends its meaning, the novelist and the reader of fiction share another kind of language.

Vocabulary

1. wrought (3)—created, shaped, formed, devised, or made happen
2. nominalized (13)—converted into nouns
3. converses (7)—talks to or with, makes conversation
4. astonished (13)—stunned, surprised
5. impeccable (13)—without flaw
6. benign (14)—kind, gracious, unharmful
7. insular (15)—isolated or removed from
8. semantic (16)—related to meaning in language, a theory of meaning
9. nascent (20)—beginning to exist, the process of being born
10. quandary (20)—predicament, state of indecision
11. wittily (20)—with humor and knowledge

Chapter 28
Exposition: Causal Analysis, p. 653

■ **"The Teacher Who Changed My Life" by Nicholas Gage—p. 653**

Questions on Content, Structure, and Style

1. What is Gage's stated purpose in writing this essay? Are there other purposes as well?
2. According to Gage, what was Miss Hurd's greatest gift to him? What cause and effect relationship does this essay explore?
3. Gage's essay covers many years—nearly his lifetime, in fact. Why is this broad span of time important to his message?
4. What key scene best captures the essence of Gage's regard for Miss Hurd and her effect on his life? Explain your choice.
5. Are there any details given that are not vital to the central idea of the essay? Explain your selections.
6. Often, a key component of causal analysis essays is description. Choose two examples of effective description and indicate two sections of the essay in which the reader might want more descriptive detail.
7. There are two key uses of dialogue in this essay. Find these sections and explain why Gage may have chosen to emphasize these particular moments, rather than others, with dialogue.
8. Consider Gage's use of transitions between paragraphs, listing examples of smooth transitions and noting those that are more abrupt.
9. Gage uses several examples of Miss Hurd's behavior to illustrate her character. What traits emerge in the following paragraphs: 6, 8, 11, 15, 16, 17, 18, and 22? Why is this a more effective way of revealing her character to the reader than simply telling the audience what she was like?
10. How does this essay illustrate the advice given by Alex Haley in his essay "Thank You" that appears in Chapter 23?

Answers to Questions

1. Gage concludes his essay by stating that it is a tribute to Marjorie Hurd, but his larger purpose is to tell a broad audience how a teacher can make a dramatic difference in someone's life.
2. Her greatest gift to Gage was "direct[ing] [his] grief and pain into writing," giving him a new interest that was to change his life and goals. Miss Hurd (the cause) inspired him to hone his writing skills (effect) and steered him toward writing about his family (effect), which led to Gage's career as a writer and journalist (effect).
3. Gage's goal is to show how Miss Hurd changed his life and this can only be accomplished if readers are allowed to see her continuing influence on him as he matures personally and professionally.
4. There are a number of possible answers to this question but because of its detail and emotional impact, the most likely choice is the portion presented in paragraphs 8–12 where Gage discusses writing about leaving Greece. Readers are allowed to see through Gage's eyes how Miss Hurd's prompting had a powerful impact on him.
5. Here, too, answers will vary. Some students might feel that the details of family celebrations are irrelevant (the music, the food, the dancing) while others might argue that all of Gage's

descriptions are appropriate to the focus of his essay. Debate on this subject will help students clarify their own views of the relationship between essay focus and development.

6. Student responses will vary.

7. Gage uses dialogue twice: when he first introduces Miss Hurd (this allows his readers to "hear" her just as he did, making her real to his audience) and when Miss Hurd calls after President Reagan's mention of Gage's mother (here she is seen as caring and warm, a contrast to her earlier words that round out his characterization of her).

8. There are any number of smooth, effective transitions that students might cite. Some more abrupt shifts include the transition between paragraphs 14 and 15 as well as 16 and 17, and 20 and 21.

9. Paragraph 6 reveals her toughness, paragraph 8 her insight, paragraph 11 her pride and kindness; paragraph 15 shows her devotion, paragraph 16 her persistence, paragraphs 17 and 18 her compassion and thoughtfulness, paragraph 22 her deep regard for Gage. If Gage had told his readers she possessed these traits, rather than showing Miss Hurd in action, her portrait would not be as vivid.

10. Haley urges readers to thank those people who have made a significant contribution to their lives. (Teachers may wish to pair these essays in advance of an essay assignment that asks students to write about an influential person.)

Vocabulary

1. refugee (1)—displaced person
2. portly (2)—plump
3. layabouts (6)—lazy people
4. honed (7)—sharpened
5. Iron Curtain (9)—political and ideological barrier isolating an area
6. mortified (11)—humiliated
7. balky (16)—hesitant, uncooperative
8. serpentine (19)—snakelike
9. void (20)—emptiness
10. bounty (21)—abundance, plenty
11. testament (21)—tribute
12. catalyst (21)—agent causing an action
13. emphatically (21)—strongly, vehemently
14. eulogy (22)—informal statement of tribute to someone delivered after his or her death

■ "Mystery!" by Nicholas Meyer—p. 657

Questions on Content, Structure, and Style

1. According to Meyer, who enjoys reading mystery novels?
2. What is Meyer's thesis? How does he support his thesis?
3. Meyer states in paragraph eight that "life is an anarchic proposition in which meaningless events conspire daily to alter our destiny without rhyme or reason." Why might reading mysteries be particularly useful to readers in contemporary society?
4. Figurative language can help glue a text together via the extended metaphor. Find and interpret several examples of figurative language.
5. On what point do Meyer and the "highfalutin apologists of the detective genre" disagree?
6. In paragraph 9, what does the author mean when he refers to a highly stylized literary formula? How does this formula contribute to the reader's enjoyment of the mystery? What are other formulas used in literature?

7. How do the characters Sherlock Holmes, Philip Marlowe, Miss Marple, and Columbo mentioned in paragraph 10 fit into Meyer's argument?
8. What key descriptions persuade readers of Meyer's essay to read mystery novels?
9. Discuss Meyer's use of colloquial language and clichés. Are they appropriate for his audience?
10. Meyer is attempting to explain the causes of the mystery story's popularity. Compare your thoughts on the causes (or effects) of some other popular-culture trend to the ideas of your classmates.

Answers to Questions

1. Meyer states that mystery novels have universal appeal and are enjoyed by readers of all races, genders, ages, national origins, and financial status.
2. Meyer contends that reading mysteries is comforting and restful. He states that a variety of readers seek and find comfort in the mystery because, unlike real life, in mystery stories, the bad guy is caught or identified and all the "loose ends" are tied up.
3. Swapping the stresses of the poor economy, the weak job market, and our country's contentious political landscape for the solvability of a mystery novel may be especially appealing to contemporary audiences.
4. Possible examples include: "curl up" (4), "As sure as God made little green apples, it all adds up to something" (7), "lowering cloud" (8). Curling up with a good book describes the reading process and the other two examples refer to the events in mystery novels.
5. According to Meyer, the "highfalutin apologists'" belief that readers of mystery novels find satisfaction in "following the clues along with the detective" is "pretentious and tenuous." Meyer maintains that readers actually prefer the *illusion* of participation, gaining more pleasure from the stories' tidy endings than from attempting to solve the crimes themselves.
6. Meyer is referring to the structured plotline mystery writers follow; readers may find comfort in the novel's formulas and reliability. Other highly stylized literary forms include Joseph Campbell's monomyth, the sonnet, and the haiku.
7. These characters, well-known to any reader of classic detective novels, give audiences someone to root for, a hero. These characters appeal to audiences because they are steady and reassuring; if there is a criminal, these characters will catch him/her. It is the stability that these characters provide that contributes to the success of the mystery genre.
8. Responses will vary; students will likely comment on scenes evoking feelings of coziness and contentment, such as "curling up" with a book or enjoying a neat solution to a complicated situation.
9. Such diction ("this stuff," "things that go bump in the night," "little green apples") gives Meyer's essay a light, folksy tone, probably all right for an essay in *TV Guide* dedicated to a discussion of fun reading. Some readers may argue that Meyer's language is a parody of the kind of stock plots and language often found in mysteries themselves.
10. Students might compare ideas on popular video games, fashions, television shows, or movies. Why, for example, is tattooing popular with young people? Why -- at this writing -- is there a glut of books, TV shows, and movies about vampires?

Vocabulary

1. conjunction (4)—the act of conjoining; combination
2. connote (5)—to signify or suggest (certain meanings, ideas, etc.)
3. mayhem (6)—random or deliberate violence
4. anarchic (8)—advocating anarchy; lawless
5. highfalutin (11)—pompous; haughty
6. pretentious (12)—characterized by assumption of dignity or importance
7. tenuous (12)—thin in consistency; unsubstantial

■ "Cell Phones and Social Graces" by Charles Fisher—p. 659

Questions on Content, Structure, and Style

1. Why does Fisher begin his essay insisting he is not a Luddite?
2. How is this essay developed by causal analysis?
3. What, in addition to explanation of his personal choice, is Fisher's larger purpose?
4. Characterize Fisher's tone in this essay. Humorous? Hostile? Something else?
5. What might be the purposes of paragraphs 2 and 3 in terms of Fisher's argument?
6. How does Fisher most often support and clarify his claims about cell phone users' lack of social graces?
7. How does Fisher's word choice help the reader "see" the many scenes he describes?
8. In what way does the conclusion return to Fisher's thesis?
9. Do you agree or disagree with Fisher's point of view? Does he have a valid point or does he go too far in his criticism?
10. In your opinion, are there other technologies that today encourage negative behavior as well as offering benefits? Can you offer examples to support your view?

Answers to Questions

1. Fisher wants his audience to know that he is not against all technological advances, that he is not an extremist who balks at progress.
2. Fisher explains the reasons he does not own a cell phone, including his desire for privacy and his frustration with the quality and pricing. But his main reason is that he fears he will become one of the discourteous, enslaved cell phone users that he sees everywhere around him.
3. Through his criticism of the bad manners and insensitivity displayed by some cell phone users, Fisher asks readers to examine and, if appropriate, improve their own behavior.
4. Some readers will thoroughly enjoy Fisher's tone, finding his use of sarcasm, irony, and hyperbole ("social Troglodytes") humorous and vivid; others may be offended or even antagonized by the extent of his disdain. It's quite possible, given the audience for whom this essay was originally written, that Fisher purposefully used exaggeration to encourage spirited responses "and argument" from his student-readers, most of whom are cell phone users. (Swift's famous ironic essay "A Modest Proposal," presented in Chapter 32, might be worth mentioning here.)
5. Fisher employs the argumentative technique of first conceding some value to the opposition's position "amazing creations…good reasons to own a cell phone" before he moves on to showing why his point of view is the better one.
6. Many personal examples illustrate his claims throughout the essay: bookstore woman (3), sons (5), biking (6), woman in the park (8), Safeway shopper (9), movie theater (10), Disney World (11), student at Commencement (13), funeral (14), Bible study (14), and others.
7. Fisher uses action verbs ("cell phone impaled in her ear"), vivid modifiers ("lady bobbing on a carousel stallion"), sensory details ("urgent bee-vibration"), figurative language ("intruding like unwanted aliens"), and specific brand and place names ("'foot remedies' aisle at Walgreens") to help recreate the scenes for his readers. Students should see many other examples of descriptive diction.
8. The conclusion returns to Fisher's personal choice, and he also acknowledges that not everyone who owns a cell phone has to become enslaved to it. He "likely wouldn't" and, for that very reason, doesn't need a cell phone.
9. This essay should provoke lively discussion, with some students protesting that Fisher over-generalizes, basing his case on the actions of a few rude people. Others will see merit in his call for improved manners and consideration of others.

10. Students might, for example, mention social networking sites such as Facebook, whose critics claim too often substitute for real personal interaction. Is phone messaging most often helpful or a waste of time–is Twitter fritter?

Vocabulary

1. tootled (1)—a gentle, repeated tooting sound
2. troglodytes (7)—cave dweller
3. slavish (8)—excessively dependent, enslaved
4. decorum (13)—dignity or good taste
5. odious (14)—inspiring hatred, contempt, or disgust
6. cornucopia (15)—symbol of abundance

129

Chapter 29
Argumentation, p. 663

■ A Scientist: "I Am the Enemy" by Ron Kline—p. 663

Questions on Content, Structure, and Style

1. Why does Kline begin with the first, provocative line?
2. What is the author's thesis regarding the use of laboratory animals?
3. What examples of medical advances from animal research does Kline offer as evidence to support this thesis?
4. Why does Kline refer to several major arguments frequently used against animal experimentation? What is the main reason he disagrees with anti-experimentation activists?
5. How does Kline refute the argument that computer simulation is a legitimate alternative to experimentation?
6. How does the author use emotional appeals? Are they effective?
7. What concessions does the author make to show he does understand that activists have sometimes had legitimate concerns?
8. Describe Kline's tone. How does he try to gain the confidence of a skeptical reader?
9. Kline claims that a "vocal but misdirected minority" has had too much influence on politicians and legislation. Do you agree with his assessment? What is the majority opinion? What current issues are often influenced by the strong voices of minorities? What historical issues have been subject to the strong influence of a minority? Is it good or bad that minorities can have such impact?
10. Is Kline's overall argument convincing? How could you make it more so? How might you argue against the essay?

Answers to Questions

1. Kline's blunt statement identifying himself as the enemy and the explanation of why he devotes his professional life to research personalize the opposition. Animal rights activists might find a villainous, heartless opponent more to their liking because it is much easier to demonize a vicious enemy. Kline's opening takes the fire out of that type of illogical and personal attack, and he turns the argument toward the reasonable purposes for using animals in the laboratory.
2. Kline believes animal research is essential to the continued development of new therapies and innovative surgeries. He criticizes both the public and his peers involved in medical research for not defending what he believes is a legitimate and ethical practice.
3. In paragraph 7, Kline explains that vaccines, antibiotics, drugs, and advanced surgical procedures have been developed with animal research. (Students should be asked if these are specific or hypothetical. How do they know? How could Kline make these examples far more convincing?)
4. When he acknowledges the major arguments of those opposed to animal research, he shows an understanding of their viewpoint. By doing so, he has the opportunity to explain why those viewpoints are not correct. His major point for his side of the argument is that human lives can be saved, and human pain and suffering can be diminished with the technology and other medical knowledge from continued experimentation on animals. He believes this probable outcome is a higher value than any suffering inflicted on the animals.

5. He explains that computer-simulated models cannot be as productive in medical research as they are in other sciences because of the inexactness of medicine and the complexity of biological systems.

6. Kline uses emotional appeals effectively to encourage the reader to apply the same kind of sympathy they might have for research animals to human beings in tragic medical circumstances. At the beginning of the essay, he compels the reader to see him as a humane researcher motivated by his concern for "healthy, happy children." In paragraph 3, he argues that those on his side of the argument might have allied the public more closely had they resorted to the same types of emotional appeals as animal activists by "waving equally sad posters of children dying of leukemia or cystic fibrosis." The next paragraph cites other examples of children in tragic accidents; using children rather than the elderly with Parkinson's, for example, is calculated to pull at the reader's emotions. As he concludes (paragraph 8), he once more reminds readers that his opinions come from his watching "many children die, and their parents grieve," and charges them to have as much compassion for dying humans as they would for a dog or cat.

7. In paragraph 5, Kline does agree that computer simulation has some value, principally to offer technological models. In his concluding paragraph, he admits that activists have improved conditions for experimental animals and that they have encouraged scientists to use suitable alternatives.

8. Throughout the essay, Kline's tone is reasonable and nonthreatening. He shows respect for his opposition rather than attempting to ridicule them; he gives activists credit in his conclusion for bringing attention to the humane treatment of animals involved in research.

9. Student responses will vary.

10. Students might add more detailed evidence of the many treatments and therapies that have been developed by using animal research, and evidence to substantiate that animals are indeed treated humanely in laboratory experiments. Those arguing against the essay might be reminded to maintain the reasonableness of their arguments, as has Kline, rather than resorting to purely emotional arguments. (To broaden the discussion of animal rights, teachers might pair this essay with the PETA ad that appears in Chapter 10.)

Vocabulary

1. vilified (1)—made evil or sinful
2. inhumane (1)—cruel, brutal
3. simulation (2)—imitation, false resemblance
4. apathetic (2)—unfeeling
5. unconscionably (3)—unreasonably
6. malevolent (4)—wishing evil to others
7. placate (6)—to quiet or soothe anger

■ "Defining the SAT Downward" by the Editorial Board of *USA Today*—p. 665

Questions on Content, Structure, and Style

1. What is the editorial board's thesis?
2. What are the editorial board's main points?
3. What is the purpose of the salad bar metaphor in paragraph seven? How does figurative language contribute to the persuasive tone of the editorial?
4. What organizational pattern does the editorial use (see Chapter 10)?
5. How does the editorial board support its arguments in paragraphs 4 and 5?
6. Which point in this essay do you find the most persuasive? The least? Why?

7. What does the editorial board recommend in place of the new College Board policy? How might this recommendation be strengthened?
8. For colleges with entrance requirements, which parts of a student's application be weighted most? Grades, test scores, writing samples, class ranking, teachers' recommendations? Should colleges consider such factors as financial need, gender or racial identity, or family educational background in their acceptances?

Answers to Questions

1. The editorial board objects to the College Board's new Score Choice policy for SAT takers.
2. The editorial board feels that this policy favors economically advantaged test takers who can afford to take the SAT numerous times and then send only their best score to their target choices. The *USA Today* editors feel that this policy also "harms the integrity of the SAT by reducing the amount of information colleges are getting about applicants' abilities" (2). Additionally, the editorial board fears that the Score Choice policy encourages students to play the "game," rather than actually reflecting a student's academic ability. Finally, the editorial board voices concern that students will continue to try to purchase diagnoses of learning disabilities in order to gain extra time during the test. This will lead to a further decline in the test's integrity.
3. The editorial board fears that the Score Choice program will lead to further decline in the integrity of the SAT as a measure of academic ability. The salad bar metaphor, including phrases such as "sprinkling" and "garnishing," conveys disdain for the current Score Choice program and foreshadows further decline of the SAT.
4. The essay most closely follows Pattern B (see page 291). The editorial describes the College Board's new policy and the College Board's reason for implementing the policy; then the authors offer evidence refuting the College Board's claims.
5. The editorial board uses statistics to support its criticisms in these paragraphs, to counter the SAT board's claim that they provide lower-income students with waivers and to argue that there is abuse of the policy for students with learning disabilities.
6. Most students agree that repetition of the test-taking raises scores, and some will argue that picking the best results does provide the truest measure of their skills. Some will question whether the editorial board's use of statistics regarding lower-income students is relevant; the waivers are there and perhaps the additional 170,000 didn't wish to apply for them. The rise in the number of students claiming disability may have less to do with finding a "loophole" than with more accurate diagnosis and reporting. Some students may also bristle at the "either-or" choice in the concluding paragraph.
7. The editorial board wants the College Board to use "proven gauges of academic success, such as the standardized essay-writing portion and tests on advanced-level subjects" (6). The editorial board might offer some research data to support their claim that these particular tests are "proven gauges."
8. Answers will vary and might lead to interesting panel discussions or individual argumentative essays. Students might research some of the many other controversial issues surrounding standardized testing and college entrance criteria.

Vocabulary

1. bias (2)—a preference or inclination
2. garnish (7)—a substance used as an embellishment or decoration on a prepared drink or food dish

Questions on Content, Structure, and Style

1. What is Gainley's thesis? Where is it located? Is this an appropriate place for it? Why?
2. On what premises does Gainley build her essay?
3. Where does Gainley address the opposition?
4. To what does the author appeal in her argument?
5. What assumptions does Gainley make about how customers might view tattoos and body piercings?
6. Gainley argues that attitudes toward new trends will change with continued exposure to those trends. On what does she base this assumption? Could she have strengthened this part of the argument? How?
7. Does Gainley make concessions to the opposition? Where?
8. Trace the organization of the argument through each paragraph.
9. How does the tone of the essay contribute to the author's purpose?
10. Are you persuaded by Gainley's argument? How might you respond to her?

Answers to Questions

1. "No organization should have to change to accommodate a candidate . . . as long as its standards are legal" (paragraph 10).
2. Premise 1: That we make assumptions about people based on appearances, which is the very argument the opposition claims is unfair. Premise 2: Employers must hire candidates that will not scare away customers. Therefore, the candidate for a job must change or choose a profession that accepts him or her as is.
3. The opposition is addressed in paragraphs 3, 4, 6, and 9. In 3, she addresses the maxim "You can't judge a book by its cover," which we can only assume was posited in the argument she is trying to refute (the high school editorial). In 4, she asserts that covers are intended to reveal, and in fact rely on people making assumptions. In 6, she addresses arguments that may have been made or could be made about freedom and discrimination and legality. In 9, she appeals to the opposition's belief in freedom.
4. In 9, she appeals to emotion and logic in the direct appeal to ideas of freedom and fairness. But she also appeals to reader's fear of not finding employment.
5. Gainley's first premise assumes that all people, which would include all customers, make assumptions based on appearances. Second, from this she assumes that because of this an unnamed number would take their business elsewhere. Third, she assumes that the number would be sufficient to negatively affect profits. Fourth, she assumes that profit outweighs expression. Students may find others.
6. She bases this assumption on one example—women wearing pants. She makes no distinctions between dress and permanent changes, such as tattoos. She could have strengthened this part of the argument by addressing that a tattoo, while a permanent adornment, is an enhancement made by choice. As such, it does not fall under the category of a "factor an applicant can't control." Students may have other opinions.
7. Her main concession comes in paragraph 1 when she states that "Every person has a need to be accepted," in paragraph 8 when she states we have the right to make personal choices, and in 9 when she states that those choices express whom we are.
8. The argument is traced thus: 1—Introduction orients reader to topic of job search and personal choice. 2—addresses idea of acceptance, references back to high school and thus audience of job seekers, sets up a problem, and expands it to include body piercing and hairstyles. 3—Addresses the opposition's argument that "you can't judge a book by its cover" and attempts to refute it by

asserting that covers are intended to reveal, and in fact rely on, people making assumptions. 4—Expands to include the idea that whole companies project an image, thereby likening companies to individuals, both of whom have choices. She uses this idea to segue into the idea of professional appearance. 5—Shifts the issue from freedom and fairness to the effects of appearance in the business world, thereby narrowing the topic and the discussion while dismissing the notion of fairness and providing a reason for judgment. 6—Addresses potential arguments about freedom, discrimination, and legality; sets up a contrast and gives an example for support and comparison. In doing so, she returns to the idea of choice. 7—Provides personal testimony as evidence/support/authority on the subject of her basic premise that employers must hire those who will project their image so as to not scare away customers. 8—Argues that trends that continue will, over time, alter people's perceptions and that negative attitudes will shift to newer trends. This paragraph transitions back to the idea of consequences but now places the focus clearly on people that do not conform to expectations. 9—Restates the premises of the argument. 10—Concludes that the individual must change, not the organization.

9. The author's tone is for the most part reasonable. She sounds most disingenuous in paragraph 7 when she states that while she may not have "issues with visible tattoos or piercings," she cannot count on her customers not to have any biases.

10. Answers will vary. Students with piercings and tattoos may have strong opinions and personal stories regarding employment to share. (Teachers might consider pairing this essay with "Poem for an Inked Daughter," which appears in Chapter 34.)

Chapter 30
Description, p. 669

■ **"A Day at the Theme Park" by W. Bruce Cameron—p. 669**

Questions on Content, Structure, and Style

1. What is the tone of this essay and when did you first recognize it?
2. What is Cameron's purpose and thesis? Is his thesis stated or implied?
3. What audience(s) might most appreciate Cameron's essay?
4. What sensory details does Cameron use to help readers share his feeling towards the park?
5. Where does Cameron use hyperbole or exaggeration for comic effect?
6. How does Cameron use sentence construction in paragraph 4 to emphasize a point about the theme park's food?
7. Why does Cameron use "you" instead of "I" in his essay, even though the experience he is describing is his own?
8. How does Cameron's last paragraph conclude the essay's narrative structure? Is this ending consistent with the essay's general tone?

Answers to Questions

1. Cameron's essay is humorous; if students don't catch the tone in the very first line (a weekend at a theme park on the list of kids' list of life's necessities), they almost surely will see the comic irony of sentence two, in which Cameron describes a theme park as the place in which "you can enjoy all your favorite pastimes at once, such as motion sickness and heat exhaustion."
2. Cameron writes to entertain his newspaper readers. His thesis, though not directly stated, is that theme parks are wretched places for parents, who grin-and-bear the agony for their children who enjoy them.
3. Parents who have shared Cameron's experience may smile widely in recognition, but any readers who hate amusement parks (and have been dragged there by friends or family) can identify.
4. Sensory details (the boiling sun, the stomach-compressing and plummeting rides, the shouting attendants, the nasty food, and so on) help readers see, feel, and hear the people and things at what Cameron calls "this hellish place" (6).
5. Cameron uses comic exaggeration throughout the essay; perhaps the best line is "Food at a theme park is so expensive it would be cheaper to just eat your own money" (4). Other examples include references to "the boiling point of tennis shoes" (2), the attendants' use of pepper spray (3), ingredients of the food (4), the post-ride loss of his face (6), and his "one regret" that he will not have an opportunity to punish his children for bringing him to the park (6).
6. He uses parallelism, repeating the phrase "which is sugar" to emphasize the unhealthful nature of theme park food.
7. Cameron uses "you" to pull his readers along for the ride. The use of the second-person pronoun universalizes the experience, from that of one parent to many.
8. The essay began describing the morning arrival at the park (paragraph 2) and humorously concludes with their departure at the end of their day. Cameron has "survived" the park ordeal and, therefore, nothing scares him now, not even wild and crazy teenage driving.

Vocabulary

1. endearing (1)—being held in affection; being valued highly
2. fiendish (2)—a person displaying great wickedness; or the quality of intense pursuit, as in fanatical
3. discourteous (3)—not polite
4. acrophobia (5)—a fear of heights
5. impervious (7)—cannot be affected by

■ "The Way to Rainy Mountain" by N. Scott Momaday—p. 670

Questions on Content, Structure, and Style

1. Momaday's narrator is clearly reminiscing, but of what?
2. Momaday seamlessly blends time, shifting from era to era as though it is all one memory. What does this technique add to your understanding of the journey taking place?
3. What does Momaday mean in paragraph one by "the prairie is an anvil's edge" and how does this knowledge fit into his theme of rebirth?
4. Momaday's use of figurative language permeates his descriptions. Discuss the effects of the following: "the steaming foliage seems almost to writhe in fire" (1), "they entered the world through a hollow log" (4), "they were bent and blind in the wilderness" (6), "clouds that sail . . . are shadows that move upon the grain like water, dividing light" (7).
5. Where do you find some examples of personification and how do they contribute to the piece?
6. "Here and there on dark stones were ancestral names (15). What other lines in the story are echoed here?
7. What is the function of paragraph 11?
8. The narrator retells the "legend at the base of the rock"—Devil's Tower—in paragraph 8. He then states that "so long as the legend lives the Kiowas have kinsmen in the night sky." To what exactly is he referring and how does it work into the frame story?
9. In paragraph 14, Momaday juxtaposes the smallness of his grandmother's house and the giant size of the cricket that "filled the moon like a fossil." To what is he referring in the line that follows: "It had gone there, I thought, to live and die, for there of all places, was its small definition made whole and eternal."
10. In the final paragraph the author writes, "Looking back once, I saw the mountain and came away." Why is this visit to the grave so brief?

Answers to Questions

1. The narrator is reminiscing about the following: his grandmother (3, 4, 5, 9, 10); his people (3, 4, 6, 7, 8, 9, 12, 13); the land of his ancestors (2, 7, 8, 15); his own travels (6, 7, 8); his childhood (10, 12, 13); and his grandmother's house (1 and 14). In paragraph 11 he is not reminiscing.
2. Responses will vary but some discussion should ensue about its being more than a physical journey to visit a grave. This is a spiritual ancestral memory brought to light in writing. It pays tribute to the author's people, acknowledging grief and suffering as equal challenges to spirit and survival. His grandmother's death provides the impetus for the journey, which then becomes the vehicle for transforming grief and comprehending its role in the larger journey of life. There is a theme of rebirth into new understanding and giving new life to the past by conveying stories from the past.
3. In this metaphor the prairie is likened to an anvil's edge. The anvil, used to shape iron in the presence of fire, represents the unyielding heat of the prairie at Rainy Mountain where the

"hardest weather in the world is" (4). Momaday comes back to this idea repeatedly, suggesting that those who can survive it are strong.

4. Responses will vary. Having students deal with explaining how they are affected will help them connect more closely to the text and come to comprehend Momaday's connection to earth more clearly. Not all students will have experiential knowledge of the rural and wild earth that Momaday reveals and, therefore, a general discussion on this question may help broaden horizons, so to speak.

5. Personification is abundant in paragraph seven: "Sweet clover takes hold of the hills," "the sun is at home on the plains," the oldest deity (Sol) ranging after the solstices," and one not quite as easy to see involves the "northern winter" as a mother figure when her progeny move south and must "wean" themselves from her climate.

6. These words take us directly back to paragraph 11: "They stand *here* and *there* against the sky . . . ." References to his ancestors are clear in the final paragraph, but now we can clarify the meaning of the sentinel houses in paragraph 11.

7. Paragraph 11 functions to shift the story from his ancestor's memories to his own childhood memories by using the houses on the plains as a metaphor for his ancestors. When he states that "you approach them for a longer time than you expect," he entreats the reader to participate in his movement through time, asking us, if you will, to see life and death as universal experiences but also shifting us to his own memories.

8. He refers directly to the Big Dipper, which is associated with the North Star and navigation. From this we understand that his ancestors discovered how to leave the northern mountains and travel south. Devil's Tower probably functioned as a compass, of sorts. Moreover, with "kinsmen in the night sky" the Kiowas acknowledged themselves as part of the universe they traversed, and it of them. In this way, the telling of the legend passes along a belief system to succeeding generations. The retelling here functions to explain that "story" is strong in passing along traditions, but it also teaches that if one follows the path of tradition, one can find one's way out of darkness. This idea is key to the frame story of a pilgrimage begun in grief and ended in acceptance.

9. The "It" in this sentence would seem to refer to the cricket and may do so on one level of understanding in which he imagines the cricket as part of the universe that extends beyond mortality. But we might also read this passage to refer to "His line of vision," for then we can connect his sense of "seeing with the mind's eye" (5) what his grandmother had known about Rainy Mountain and what he eventually left with—an understanding of his own place in the chain of ancestors and the universe itself.

10. The journey's destination was not the place but the alteration of spirit and mind. He had attained that the night before. Physical completion of the trek ended at the grave, but the grave itself had no more compulsion than the houses on the plain, for death is not something one seeks and understanding of it is best left to time.

Vocabulary

1. anvil (1)—a large piece of iron used by blacksmiths to forge iron into various shapes
2. writhe (1)—to wriggle and sway
3. preeminently (3)—first and foremost
4. disposition (3)—a person's tendency toward a particular type of behavior
5. stores (3)—provisions—food and other items that sustain life
6. awful (8)—full of awe, reverence, or amazement
7. tenuous (8)—sketchy, not certain
8. deicide (9)—the erasure (murder) of a deity or god in the minds or actions of a people
9. ample (12)—plentiful or large
10. enmities (12)—feelings of ill will toward another

11. mourning (14)—a period of grief or sadness for the loss of a loved one
12. scissortail (15)—bird, specifically a flycatcher, with a deeply forked tail
13. hied (15)—fled quickly

■ "Walking on the Moon" by David R. Scott—p. 675

Questions on Content, Structure, and Style

1. What is Scott's thesis and is it stated directly or implied?
2. What is the tone of the first half of this piece? What words or phrases contribute to these feelings?
3. Identify some sensory details included in the passage.
4. How does the use of imagery contribute to Scott's thesis?
5. Who is Scott's audience?
6. Scott is describing a landscape totally unfamiliar to all but a select handful of people. How does he help his readers understand what he is seeing?
7. How does Scott's tone change in paragraph 16?
8. How does Scott describe earth? What are his implications about our planet?
9. What is symbolic about the offerings Scott and his fellow explorers leave for future astronauts?
10. What does Scott mean when he describes the moon as a "radiant body where man has taken his first steps into a frontier that will never end" (20)?

Answers to Questions

1. Scott's implied thesis is that walking on the moon was a beautiful, life-changing experience.
2. Scott's tone in the first half of the essay is reverent, awe-struck, and amazed. Phrases such as "stars spangled the sky with their distant icy fire" (3), "dazzled our eyes," (3), "the wonderland of the lunar surface," (7), and "the moon becomes a friendlier place" (14) contribute to the essay's astonished tone.
3. The essay contains numerous details related to sight: "the sun exploded into our view" (3) and "everything the color of milk chocolate" (4); smell: "a pervasive odor, similar to that of gunpowder" (15); touch: "ease of strolling on a trampoline" (9); and sound: "purr of the [oxygen] machines (13).
4. Scott's detailed, poetic descriptions capture his sense of amazement at the moon's surface and his opportunity to walk on the moon. The ornate descriptions help readers recognize the event as a remarkable experience.
5. The essay was originally written for *National Geographic*, so the reader can assume that the piece was intended for readers with an interest in science, nature, and the environment. Space travel has a broad appeal to many readers.
6. In additional to the sensory details discussed previously, Scott offers specific objective information (e.g., the height of the mountains, the temperature, the gravitational pull). He often compares the unfamiliar to the familiar so that readers may imagine the scene: a line on the mountains looks like "a bathtub ring" (8); moon dust has the consistency of "coal dust and talcum power" (12); the moon walker accepts falling like a child (11).
7. Scott's tone is serious and subdued in paragraph 16 when he addresses the possibility that humans will not revisit the moon for a very long time.
8. Scott describes earth as "so blue, so beautiful, so beloved. And so bedeviled…" (16). Scott and his crew hope that technology capable of space travel can solve some of the earth's problems in the areas of ecological imbalance, world hunger, and energy shortage.
9. Scott and the other astronauts leave two plaques, one with two hemispheres of earth, the spacecraft's name, date of mission, and a crew roster; the other with the names of all fourteen (Russian and American) astronauts who have died in space exploration. They also leave

138

footprints, a falcon feather, a four-leaf clover, a Bible, and a figurine of an astronaut. Scott believes future astronauts will see these items as evidence that earthlings were curious, intelligent, and thoughtful beings. The LM, figurine, and footprints are clues as to the physical aspects of Scott and his fellow astronauts, while the feather and clover represent the connection to nature. The Bible signifies religious faith.

10. This line suggests that although travel to the moon may be temporarily suspended, there are still infinite possibilities for future space travel.

Vocabulary

1. tumult (1)—violent and noisy commotion
2. girded (1)—to encircle; surround; enclose
3. sector (2)—part of a circle
4. impenetrable (3)—impossible to get in or through
5. corona (3)—a type of plasma atmosphere of the sun
6. zenith (5)—the point of a celestial sphere vertically above a given position or observer
7. tableau (7)—picture, as of a scene
8. nil (11)—nothing or zero
9. mantles (12)—something that covers, envelopes, or conceals
10. acrid (15)—sharp or biting to the taste or smell
11. hiatus (16)—a gap or pause in time
12. fauna…flora (18)—animals…plants

Chapter 31
Narration, p. 679

■ **"38 Who Saw Murder Didn't Call the Police" by Martin Gansberg—p. 679**

Questions on Content, Structure, and Style

1. Does Gansberg's article have a thesis? What is it?
2. What point of view does Gansberg use? Who tells the story? What advantages and/or limitations does his narrative choice present?
3. In some ways Gansberg's article is a factual newspaper account of the Genovese incident; in other ways it seems more like fiction. Explain his technique.
4. Evaluate Gansberg's tone in this essay. What seems to be his attitude toward his subject?
5. Note the modifiers—especially the adverbs—that Gansberg uses when he records the statements of the witnesses. What does his choice of words reveal about these people?
6. What, apparently, were Gansberg's main sources for the facts of the Genovese case?
7. How does Gansberg structure his essay? What organizational pattern does he employ?
8. Why does Gansberg include the two paragraphs about the arrest of the suspect? Is the information given here necessary to the point he's trying to make? Does it add to the story?
9. What effect does the material presented in paragraphs 11–16 have? How can Gansberg know these details? Is this a good tactic for writers of descriptive essays?
10. What reason might Gansberg have for including the information about the cost of the homes in the neighborhood where the incident occurred? Is this relevant? Why or why not?

Answers to Questions

1. Whether the article has a thesis in the usual sense of the word is debatable, but it certainly presents a point of view. Gansberg is appalled by individuals so fearful of "getting involved" that they will stand by and watch while their fellow beings are murdered.
2. He uses a third-person, omniscient narrator. The author is absent from the piece; the nameless narrator is able to recount events that could realistically not be known by the author, except secondhand. However, he tells the story as though he were always present.
3. In part, Gansberg's piece is similar to the contemporary style of blending fact and fiction that some have called "faction." The story is based on fact, but Gansberg, rather than simply recording the facts, creates a short-story effect by the way he uses a narrator, records dialogue, etc.
4. Although the narrative "voice" offers no direct comment, it is clear from what is said that Gansberg is horrified by what happened and finds the incident symptomatic of a major social problem. He obviously feels compassion for Genovese and disdain for those who failed to help her.
5. He has people say things "sheepishly," "knowingly if quite casually," "without emotion." They shrug, peek out from behind partly closed doors—in short, they seem every bit as uncaring and aloof as one might expect from the facts.
6. The police and Genovese's neighbors. Most likely, his story is based, at least in part, on earlier news accounts.
7. He begins in the present, then recounts the Genovese murder in chronological order, then introduces the fact of the suspect's arrest, and closes with the witnesses' comments.

8. From the standpoint of the Genovese story and the point Gansberg is making about what happened, the material is probably unnecessary. However, from a journalistic standpoint, the material is significant and it probably answers (as well as could be expected at the time) questions most readers would ask.

9. The details could have come in part from the witnesses' accounts, but much of it is certainly fictional—Gansberg's way of dramatizing the incident and stressing the horror the victim felt. One appalling side note that instructors might point out regarding this horror felt by Genovese and other victims: in 1995 Genovese's murderer, Winston Mosely, stated to parole officials that he has suffered more than his victim because for her it was "a one-minute affair, but for the person who's caught, it's forever."

10. The facts and figures indicate that the neighborhood is upper-middle to middle-class (remember this is 1964) and composed primarily of single-family dwellings. Though Gansberg does not say so, the implication is clear: if it can happen here it can happen anywhere. These are presumably well-to-do, hard-working, successful people. Yet they failed to respond the way we might expect they should.

Vocabulary

1. recitation (4)—account, as if by rote
2. staid (6)—reserved, grave
3. distraught (26)—upset, worried

■ "Crossing the Great Divide" by Peter Fish—p. 689

Questions on Content, Structure, and Style

1. Where is South Pass, and why is it a national historical spot?
2. Why does Fish go to South Pass?
3. Why was this place so important to the wagon train settlers?
4. What does including Terry Del Bene add to Fish's narrative? How does Del Bene see South Pass?
5. Why does Fish include the diary excerpts in his essay?
6. Why, in Fish's opinion, do we "ventur[e] into the past"? What are we looking for?
7. How is Fish's son's arrival itself a "continental divide"?
8. Why does Fish want his son to see South Pass now? What image concludes this essay, and why?

Answers to Questions

1. South Pass, Wyoming, is that part of the Oregon Trail that straddles the Continental Divide, the high point of ground at which the rivers of North America flow in different directions. Without South Pass, wagon train settlers could not have easily reached the western half of the country beyond the Rocky Mountains.

2. It is the 4-month birthday of his son and Fish's own 43rd birthday, a time in life at which one looks both forward and backward. It is a mid-way point in Fish's life, just as South Pass was a mid-way point in both location and time for the settlers who were remembering the past but anticipating a new life ahead. Some of these settlers were his son's ancestors, which makes the place special to his family.

3. It was the point of no return; settlers were leaving their past lives behind and moving to the other side of their world.

4. Del Bene provides insight into the importance of South Pass, not just as the means by which to cross the mountains but as a symbol of the settlers' hopes, determination, and courage. He regards it as "almost a religious experience" (3).

141

5. The settlers' words and experiences clarify the meaning of South Pass by helping the readers see first-hand the pioneers' courage and sacrifice. Using a real person such as Charlotte Dansie puts a human face on one of the 400,000 nameless settlers, allowing readers to empathize.

6. Fisher believes that "Venturing into the past is never about the past but about the present – we look for courage and purity of intent that we cannot locate in the modern world "(12).

7. Joseph's arrival was a dramatic change for Fish; he has crossed into a new world. His new life parallels that of a settler crossing the Continental Divide: "all the rivers of my life now run in a new direction" (14).

8. He wants his son to experience (albeit not at a conscious-memory level) and honor the hopes and courage that South Pass represents, before the distractions of trivial modern life (Toys "R" Us) impinge on his childhood. Being there is a sort of baptismal event. The pioneer values associated with South Pass are the ones that Fish wants his son to carry "on his trail" – that is, on his journey through life.

Vocabulary

1. commemorate (1)—to remember through observance or celebration
2. sharpie (5)—a well-dressed man, often thought to be a con man
3. spiking (5)—embellishing; adding to make more appealing
4. embalm (5)—to protect from decay or to preserve by filling up with spices or sterilizing fluid
5. comports (6)—agrees, behaves (in relation to one's demeanor)
6. disparaged (9)—spoke about in an unkind manner
7. unflappable (13)—calm, serene

■ "Arrival at Manzanar" by Jeanne Wakatsuki Houston and James D. Houston— p. 684

Questions on Content, Structure, and Style

1. In the first paragraph of this essay the narrator describes Terminal Island as "a country as foreign as India or Arabia would have been." What does the narrator feel this way?

2. Why does the narrator's mother break her china?

3. What was Roosevelt's Executive Order 9066?

4. Why has the narrator's father "disappeared"?

5. What is the purpose of paragraph 12 in terms of educating readers who don't know about the treatment of the Japanese-Americans during World War II?

6. Paragraph 19 describes the meals served at camp and the prisoners' reactions to their food. Why are their reactions ironic?

7. What organizational pattern does Wakatsuki Houston choose and why?

8. How do moments of childhood innocence described in this story contribute to its point of view and tone?

9. Ironically, how do the Wakatsuki family's experiences compare to those of people held by the Nazis in Germany against whom our country was fighting?

10. The U.S. internment policy during this time remains controversial, with some historians acknowledging a real threat to security while others argue that racism played a key part. What is your opinion? Could such a policy be implemented today?

142

Answers to Questions

1. The narrator has lived amongst Caucasians and considers herself fully American. She does not understand why she has to move, and now that she is around other Japanese immigrants, she is confused and frightened by their customs and behaviors.

2. The mother is being forced to move and an antiques dealer tries to take advantage of her situation by offering a low price for the china. The mother has no control over moving, but she can choose whether or not to sell her china for less than what it is worth. Breaking the china symbolizes the mother's refusal to be defeated by her oppressors.

3. Roosevelt's Executive Order 9066 was a presidential order to send Japanese-Americans to internment camps. The order was issued in 1942, during World War II.

4. The narrator's father has been arrested by U. S. government officials and was held at a camp in North Dakota.

5. The narrator explains her teacher's hostility as part of the larger distrust many Americans felt toward the Japanese-Americans in California. This fear – coupled with resentment toward Japanese military forces in the Pacific – contributed to incarceration of 120,000 people of Japanese heritage in ten internment camps in seven Western states.

6. Although the prisoners are the victims of racism and prejudice, they still maintain their dignity. They do not complain about the rice dish and "dab courteously" at their food. This paragraph highlights the polite behavior so valued by Japanese culture. Ironically, the prisoners treat their captors with the respect that they themselves are denied.

7. The events are told chronologically, with readers moving with the family on their journey to Manzanar.

8. The narrator's scenes of childhood innocence, such as her "announcement" on the bus (17) and the fun of jumping on the mattress (24), relieve the sadness of this story; the narrator saw the events as a child would, with pockets of simple joy, unlike the grown-ups whose retelling of the same events would probably reflect more anger, sadness, or fear, in light of their adult understanding of the situation. The narrator's voice is remarkably free of bitterness, which encourages readers' empathy.

9. Students may see parallels in the loss of civil liberties, confiscation of property, forced transportation, identification by numbers, physical labor, and incarceration in substandard barracks surrounded by barbed wire and guards. Although certainly not death camps, the internment camps in the U.S. did share similarities with the Nazi labor camps that began in the 1930s, built upon their claim of imprisoning "enemies of the state."

10. Some students may need additional background information on this controversy. Some historians maintain that the Japanese in California were less assimilated into American society and that some still pledged allegiance to the Japanese emperor who many considered a divine being; therefore, they presented a sabotage threat. Other historians disagree, claiming that racism and financial gain from confiscated property played a big role in the policy; they point out that German-Americans were not rounded up and incarcerated but Japanese-Americans were, possibly because they looked "different" and were an easy target because of their polite demeanor. Students may debate what parts racial/cultural prejudice and "scapegoating" play in such policy; to that end, they might investigate acts of violence and vandalism against U.S. citizens of Middle Eastern heritage following the 9/11 terrorist attack.

Vocabulary

1. reign(3)—dominating power or influence
2. quiver (5)—to shake with a slight but rapid motion
3. scuttle (8)—to run with quick, hasty steps
4. internment (9)—confinement

5. patriarch (10)—the male head of the family
6. tolerance (12)—a fair, objective attitude toward those whose opinions, race, religion, etc. differ from one's own
7. barracks (17)—a large, plain building in which many people are housed
8. ominously (17)—foreboding; threatening
9. abate (23)—to reduce in amount or intensity
10. alleviate (24)—to make easier to endure

Chapter 32
Essays for Further Analysis: Multiple Strategies and Styles, p. 689

■ "I Have a Dream" by Martin Luther King, Jr.—p. 689

Questions on Content, Structure, and Style

1. King's "I Have a Dream" is a speech rather than an essay. What stylistic tactics does he use that seem especially effective for oral presentation?
2. Considering King's audience, what might be the main purpose of his speech? Is his intent to be persuasive?
3. Analyze King's opening sentence. Why is it appropriate?
4. What extended analogy does King use when discussing the Constitution and the Declaration of Independence? Is the metaphor a good one?
5. One rhetorical tactic that King employs especially well is repetition. Give examples of his use of this device. What is the effect of repetition generally? In King's speech?
6. In addition to repetition, how does King create the appealing tone of his speech?
7. King is noted for his belief in both racial harmony and nonviolent protest. Does this speech reflect that belief?
8. King quotes from both the Declaration of Independence and the song "America." What effect does this have on his message?
9. What word (and its variants) is used most often in this speech? Why is it important?
10. Is King's argument logical or emotional? Does he appeal to our minds or our hearts?

Answers to Questions

1. The most obvious device is repetition. It should be noted as well that his language is rhythmical and simple, and his sentences short and emphatic.
2. King's primary audience shared his beliefs. In this sense, the speech may be seen more as an inspirational message than persuasive discourse. But he was also reaching out to others for support of the civil rights movement.
3. The "Five score years ago" echoes the beginning of Lincoln's Emancipation Proclamation. The "great American" is Lincoln, and King is standing in the shadow of the Lincoln Memorial. The speech was given at a massive protest march celebrating the Emancipation Proclamation.
4. He compares the two documents to a check, a promissory note from the nation's founders, for the rights of freedom and justice. It is time, says King, to cash the check. His analogy is both appropriate and consistent.
5. See paragraphs 2, 4, 11–18, 20–27. Repetition is used for emphasis. In speeches it works especially well because of the limitations placed on the audience. Readers are able to follow points much more easily, for example, and can reread if necessary. King, in this speech, frequently uses extended passages in which he employs repetition—for example, the repeated phrase "I have a dream." This not only underscores his point, but also contrasts with the reality he describes.

6. King's cadence in this speech is similar to one he and other Southern ministers might use in a sermon, especially "the call" at its rousing conclusion. To lend gravitas to his words, King makes use of Biblical allusions (compare "we will not be satisfied until justice rolls down like waters and righteousness like a mighty stream" [7] to Amos 5:24; see other examples in Psalms 30:5 and Isaiah 40:4-5); other allusions recall words from familiar gospel songs ("Free at last") and Shakespeare (compare "sweltering summer of … discontent" [5] to *Richard III*'s image "winter of our discontent"). King mixes references to specific injustices (lack of fair lodging, police brutality, voting infringement) with figurative language (bank of justice, quicksands of racial injustice, solid rock of brotherhood) to motivate listeners to march on toward equality.

7. Yes. See paragraphs 6 and 7.

8. The quotes, which reflect the American ideal, offer a contrast to the American reality. King's dream is only to have that reality fulfilled. By citing lines that Americans know well and believe in, he emphasizes the point that blacks only want the rights held dear by all Americans.

9. The word is "free" (or the variant "freedom"). Freedom, of course, is the subject both of the speech and of King's "dream." Again, this speech was delivered at a celebration of the Emancipation Proclamation, which freed slaves in America.

10. Though the ideas presented are grounded in logic, the overall tone of the speech is emotional, as King tries to both inspire continuing action and assuage anger over past injustices.

Vocabulary

1. languishing (2)—without energy or spirit, weak
2. inextricably (6)—tangled, too complex to unravel

■ "Beauty: When the Other Dancer Is the Self" by Alice Walker—p. 692

Questions on Content, Structure, and Style

1. What is the significance of Walker's title? What does it mean?
2. What point of view does Walker use in this essay? Who is the narrator?
3. What verb tense is this essay written in? Where, in time, does the author "stand" in relation to the events she is describing? How does this relate to her method of organization?
4. In several instances Walker uses italics. Why? How do these passages differ from the others?
5. Why, in the first few episodes she recounts, does Walker place so much emphasis on clothing—what she wore, what people thought of her garments, etc.?
6. How does the scar change the narrator? How does this relate to the thesis, or main point, of the essay?
7. Why does Walker include the poem "On Sight" in her essay? How does it contribute to the meaning of her essay?
8. What does Walker's daughter see in the blind eye? How does this change the author's perception of her scar? herself?
9. Evaluate the final paragraph. Is this an effective conclusion? Why or why not?
10. This is obviously a personal essay, one that records a specific problem in the life of one individual. Is it more than that? Does the general theme of Walker's essay have universal application?

Answers to Questions

1. The title refers to her metaphorical quest—in the essay—for the meaning of beauty. It also refers to the incident (and the idea) related in the final paragraph. She has come to terms with her past, her other self.

2. She uses the first person. Obviously, she is writing a personal experience essay, but it might be pointed out to students that a first-person narrative does not always mean that the author and the narrator are the same person.

3. She is reflecting on past events, but she uses the present tense. This underscores the reflective nature of the essay. Notice that she uses age as a focal point for each episode and that the organization is chronological.

4. The italic passages represent the voice of the narrator in the present. Because past episodes are related in present tense as well, the italics serve to distinguish between past and present, between the old and new "self." Too, they function as transitional devices.

5. This stresses the difference between superficial, or external, beauty and the deeper beauty she comes to discover within herself.

6. The scar changes the nature of the girl completely—or, at least, she thinks so. She has not fundamentally changed, but because she has been so aware of external beauty—her clothes, her appearance, her action—she feels who she is has been radically altered. The wound makes her "blind" in more ways than one.

7. This passage is pivotal to the essay. Suddenly recalling—and confronting—the words of the doctor about the possibility of losing sight in both eyes, Walker learns, for the first time, to really see. The desert is bleak, not of interest to most people, who would say it is all the same, monotonous. Walker learns that the desert has beauty. She looks past the "flags" of vision—the symbols—and really sees. This passage provides transition from one state and time to another.

8. The child sees an image that resembles the picture of the earth taken from the moon that appears on *Big Blue Marble*. Walker has to this point been uneasy about her daughter looking at the scarred eye. When she asks, "Mommy, where did you get that world in your eye?" the pain—most of it anyway—leaves.

9. The conclusion is highly effective. It relates to the title (see question 1 above) and brings the essay full circle. The final episode is a resolution of the conflict within herself that the author recounts.

10. The essay has universal application, as most effective personal experience essays do. Readers will not have the same specific problem, but they may have some problem that creates self-doubt and dissatisfaction.

Vocabulary

1. crinolines (4)—billowing underskirts made from a stiff, starched fabric
2. boisterous (16)—rowdy

■ "A Modest Proposal" by Jonathan Swift—p. 697

Questions on Content, Structure, and Style

1. What is the "proposal" of this essay?
2. Who is speaking in this essay?
3. What is the true purpose of this essay?
4. What is meant by "irony"? Why is this essay called a "satire"?
5. At what point was it clear to you that that this essay is making a satirical point?

147

6. What are some of the narrator's main arguments for his position?
7. Why does the narrator so often use statistics in his arguments?
8. Why does the narrator often refer to the opinions of others, such as the "principled gentleman" (6), a "very knowing American" (9), and his "worthy" friend (17)?
9. How does the narrator's voice contribute to the tone and purpose of this essay?
10. Does the tradition of political satire exist today? Can you offer an example of a current political satirist?

Answers to Questions

1. The impoverished Irish, suffering under harsh English rule, could improve their economic plight and secure a number of social benefits by selling their young children for food.
2. Swift uses a first-person narrator who claims to have thought about this problem for years and has now come up with the solution, having rejected the schemes of other theorists whose "computations" he has found in error.
3. Swift wants to draw attention to the poverty and social ills of his country resulting from England's crushing treatment of the Irish.
4. Irony refers to the use of words to convey the opposite of their literal meaning and is often used to emphasis the contrast between what is said and what is meant. A satire is a literary work in which irony or wit is used to expose and/or attack folly or wickedness. In this satiric essay Swift uses irony to expose the starvation of the Irish children and the plight of their families at the hands of the "landlords" (the rich English) as well as many of the social problems that come with poverty.
5. Answers will vary, but most readers catch on pretty quickly, and almost certainly by the time the narrator claims in paragraph 9 that a healthy child at age one year makes "a most delicious, nourishing, and wholesome food, whether stewed, roasted, baked, or boiled"!
6. The narrator argues that the selling of the children for food will not only contribute to the economy but also prevent abortions, provide a variety of home-grown dishes to the rich throughout the year, decrease the number of Catholics, encourage visits to taverns, and contribute to the quality of motherhood and marriage.
7. The narrator cites the number of available children, their weights at certain times, the potential number of servings they will provide, their possible sale prices and so on, to show the economic advantage of his proposal. His figures and computations "prove" the validity of his claims.
8. The narrator frequently alludes to others (all moral and knowledgeable men, of course) who, in one way or another, offer support for his opinions, and here Swift is parodying the argumentative tactic of appealing to an authority. The narrator also uses one of the "worthy" men to introduce "a refinement" upon his scheme (17), which he is then able to refute, in imitation of another common tactic in formal argument.
9. The tone of the serious, self-righteous narrator, virtuous down to his last comments praising his lack of financial self-interest, contrasts with the absurdity of the proposal and makes Swift's irony even more delicious.
10. Political satire and irony abound today, and students may come up with many examples from a variety of sources, including *The Daily Show with Jon Stewart* and *Saturday Night Live* on television; *Doonesbury* and *Mallard Fillmore* cartoon series in newspapers; an amazing number of videos and songs available on *YouTube* and other Web sites.

Vocabulary

1. *modest (title)—inexpensive (rather than demure or chaste)
2. fricassee (9)—a stew, generally of a light colored meat in a light or brown gravy
3. ragout (9)—meat and vegetables in a thick sauce

4. *projectors (4)—schemers, those who put forth ideas
5. *parts (6)—promising abilities, talents
6. *dear (12)—expensive (in addition to cherished or kind)
7. repine (14)—complain or express dejection
8. *artificially (15)—skillfully
9. *shambles (16)—slaughterhouses
10. *distress (22)—from distraint: seizing property by legal means in order to pay debts

*Note: Some of Swift's terms carried somewhat different meanings in his day than they would for us today.

Chapter 33
Literature, p. 705

■ **"Perhaps the World Ends Here" by Joy Harjo—p. 705**

Questions on Content, Structure, and Style

1. What does the table in this poem represent?
2. What kinds of actions take place at the kitchen table as described in lines 1-9?
3. What figurative language device appears in lines 10-12? What do these lines mean, in your interpretation?
4. How has the table been a house and an umbrella?
5. At what point does the description of the table move from literal to more metaphorical? Why?
6. How does the last image in lines 20-21 provide an effective ending for this poem?
7. Harjo's poem has no rhyme scheme; how does the poem achieve unity and poetic rhythm?
8. Why does Harjo use the word "we" so often in this poem?

Answers to Questions

1. In some lines the table is just that – a literal table, one that occupies the central living space in a home. However, one may ague that the table in this poem becomes a metaphor for our common humanity – a shared bond in that we all experience joys, fears, sorrows, and hopes in our lives.
2. The poem begins simply with brief glimpses of real-life scenes common to most families: eating meals, animals under foot, teething babies, parental talks with growing children, adults gossiping and remembering.
3. The dreams are personified. Our dreams – our hopes – for our lives are so real and present they are like family members who live alongside of us: they join us at the table, drink coffee with us, hug our children, and laugh with us over our mistakes and our recoveries.
4. The table, here metaphorically representing the family life, has provided comfort in hard times, just as a house shelters against the rain and an umbrella protects from a hot sun.
5. At about mid-point the poem begins to turn; language becomes more metaphorical. By line 14, the table has come to represent the common bond of human experience through the ages: war, peace, births, deaths, universal feelings of joy, sorrow, regret, thankfulness.
6. The last lines circle back to the image of eating food – the way it has been for humans since creation -- that appears at the poem's beginning. When the world ends – whether as a single event or for each of us individually, Harjo imagines us at the table savoring the "last sweet bite" of life.
7. The poem gains unity from use of key words ("table") and similar-length stanzas, repetition of sentence structure ("We" plus verb), and rhythmic parallel construction within images ("house in the rain, an umbrella in the sun"), as well as a consistent tone. The poem's movement from the literal specifics to the metaphorical universal, from creation to extinction, carries the reader from beginning to end.
8. The use of "we" throughout the poem contributes to the notion of a shared human bond, from birth to death, from the beginning of time to its end. "We" have our own family at the kitchen table, but we also belong to the family of humankind.

■ "Ozymandias" by Percy Bysshe Shelley—p. 706

Questions on Content, Structure, and Style

1. Who is Ozymandias?
2. Who is speaking in this poem?
3. What did the traveler see in the dessert?
4. What did the traveler see in the sculptor's art?
5. What is the tone of the inscription? What does it reveal about the character of Ozymandias?
6. What is ironic about the inscription?
7. How does the concluding image of the dessert sand add to the irony?
8. What, ultimately, does Ozymandias represent to the speaker of the poem?

Answers to Questions

1. Ozymandias in this poem is a boastful ancient king who during his rule had a huge statue erected to himself. Shelley may have indeed intended this poem to be about Ramses II, the ruler of Egypt in the thirteenth century B.C. E.
2. The speaker, perhaps Shelley, is telling a story he heard from a traveler who has visited "an antique land," possibly Egypt.
3. The traveler saw a colossal statue shattered in the dessert. The legs stand upright but the face that lies nearby is shattered and half buried in the sand.
4. The traveler can see that the sculptor read the character of his haughty, self-centered king very well as he gave the face a frown, wrinkled lip, and a "sneer of cold command."
5. The inscription is the boast of a vain ruler who thinks he is the most powerful person in history; he clearly thinks his legacy will stand forever.
6. The irony comes from the contrast between the boastful ruler's belief that he and his works (his conquests, monuments, and such) will be permanently recognized and the fact that the statue is now completely destroyed by the passage of time. Nothing remains anywhere around the statue to even hint at his triumphs.
7. The desert sands, like the sands of time, have shifted and have erased the glory that once belonged to Ozymandias. The double use of alliteration ("boundless and bare" and "lone and level") in lines 11-12 emphasizes the sweep of time.
8. Ozymandias represents the vanity of the powerful who think they will be held in awe and esteem by everyone forever.

Vocabulary

1. visage (l. 4) – face
2. pedestal (l. 9) – base of a statue or column

■ "Poem for an Inked Daughter" by Jane Wheeler—p. 707

Questions on Content, Structure, and Style

1. What does "inked" mean today?
2. Who is speaking in this poem? To whom is the poem directed?
3. To what does the "it" of the first line refer? What is the purpose of the first stanza?
4. How do the words "parlor" and "gypsy" function in this poem to show generational contrasts?
5. What does the speaker "know" (l. 21) that the daughter doesn't?

6. Explain the metaphor of lines 18-19 that presents the dragon tattoo as "another gauntlet thrown down in the ongoing Mother-Daughter Wars."
7. What is the major metaphor of the poem that appears in the last six lines?
8. Where does the poet use alliteration?
9. How do the sounds of the words in the last five lines contribute to the image?
10. How does the attitude expressed in this poem contrast with that of Bonny Gainley in her essay "Judging By the Cover" (Chapter 29)? With other parents or employers you have known?

Answers to Questions

1. "Inked" is slang for tattooed.
2. The mother of a teen who has gotten a tattoo is addressing her daughter, though perhaps only in her mind rather than directly.
3. The mother rebelled against her own mother when she was young; at that time her teenage rebellion ("it") took the form of piercing her ears and wearing dangling earrings, which her strict mother regarded as low-class and inappropriate. Her own experience makes her more understanding of her daughter's actions.
4. There's word play on the contrast between the two generations' uses of the word "parlor": the Victorian parlor (formal sitting room of a house) of the mother's youth and the tattoo parlor of her daughter's. The speaker's mother called her a "dirty gypsy" in disgust, but the mother refers to her daughter as her "own gypsy girl" in a more loving acknowledgment of the teen's need to assert her independence.
5. Although the speaker's relationship with her critical mother was irreparably broken, she knows that her relationship with her daughter will be different. Even though she doesn't like her daughter's choice or their fighting, her love is ongoing and "forever permanent."
6. A gauntlet is a medieval glove that was thrown to the ground when a person was issuing a challenge to a fight. Getting a tattoo against the mother's wishes is another way in which the daughter fights against her mother's rules and values, part of the universal struggle faced by almost all mothers and teenage daughters.
7. The mother's bond of unconditional love that flows to her daughter is as strong and permanent as the lines of a tattoo that can never be removed.
8. Alliteration often unites words to form strong images in the reader's mind. Some examples here include: "defiant dragon curling dark" and "fierce fire-breathing." Repetition of sounds may affect the speed of a line, as in the quickness of "rushing red to red," which echoes pulsing blood.
9. The repetition of the "–ing" sound ("swirling, twisting") captures the notion of a tattoo flourish; the repeated "in-" sound ("intricate intimate tattoo, invisible, indelible") emphasizes the complex, not always visible, but permanent bond between the mother and her daughter.
10. The mother in this poem accepts her inked daughter "no matter what" whereas Gainley agrees that employers should be able to reject job candidates whose appearances they deem inappropriate. Figures vary, but one Harris poll estimated that 16% of all American adults today have at least one tattoo. Students may debate whether tattooing is now merely a fashion statement rather than the controversial trend it once was. All sorts of essay topics on this subject are possible, from the history of tattooing to arguments on employment policies (including bans on certain arm tattoos by the military).

Vocabulary

1. gauntlet (l. 18)—protective glove worn with medieval armor
2. indelible (l. 30)—not removable

152

Questions on Content, Structure, and Style

1. How does setting – location and weather -- contribute to this story?
2. How are the characters of Minnie and John Wright characterized? How has Minnie changed over the years?
3. At the story's beginning, how do the characters of Mrs. Hale and Mrs. Peters differ?
4. How are these women treated by Sheriff Peters and Mr. Hale? Why is the men's search for clues and motive ironic?
5. What clues to the murder do the women see?
6. What does the bird in this story symbolize?
7. Why are Mrs. Peters' comments about her kitten (243) and the death of her child (255) important?
8. At what understanding do Mrs. Peters and Mrs. Hale arrive, as described in paragraph 263? Why is this understanding crucial to this story?
9. Why is the last line of this story particularly ironic?
10. Who has become Minnie's "jury of her peers"? Do you agree with their verdict?

Answers to Questions

1. The shabby farm is isolated and repeatedly described as "lonesome" (7, three times; 25, 718), just as Minnie Wright's life is. The weather is cold and harsh, with a biting north wind; John Wright is similarly cold, later described as "a raw wind" (202).
2. Minnie was once pretty and lively, a girl who wore ribbons and liked to sing in the choir, but in the last twenty years has become more like the sagging, faded rocker (30). John is characterized as a "hard man" (202) without cheerfulness (95), one who would not install a telephone or a good stove for his wife in the isolated farmhouse.
3. Mrs. Peters is married to the sheriff and of a slightly higher social standing than Mrs. Hale; she is small and timid and in the beginning tends to defend the attitudes and actions of the men (106, 162). Mrs. Hale, a mother and a wife, feels guilty for not having visited Minnie through the years; she is more willing to defend the woman's housekeeping to the men. As someone who "hated to see things half done" (2), she first notices the strange array of the kitchen.
4. The men patronize the women (67, 76, 78, 102, 159, 279) and see women's thoughts and things as insignificant (note that the name of this story's play version is *Trifles*). The men search all around the farm for evidence but ignore the kitchen, which is just where the clues are to be found.
5. The women begin to see a pattern in the things left undone or messy; the stitching unlike the rest of Minnie's fine sewing makes them wonder what she was "nervous" about. When they discover the bird cage with a broken door and then the bird with broken neck, they begin to understand what may have happened at the Wright home. (Note, too, that early on the tidy Mrs. Hale goes about straightening up all sorts of evidence.)
6. The pretty, cheerful bird, presumably bought by Minnie for companionship, may represent Minnie herself: a pretty girl with a sweet singing voice who had been caged, silenced, and broken. However, it is John who is strangled like the bird he killed.
7. Mrs. Peters is changing: she begins to understand the rage Minnie must have felt upon John's killing of the bird, and her memories of being alone after her child died allow her to empathize with Minnie's loneliness and sadness.
8. Mrs. Peters tries to regain her composure as someone "married to the law" (282), but Mrs. Hale knows what the real crime has been. She stresses the common bond of experience among women, despite their situations or social status: "We all go through the same thing – it's all just a different kind of the same thing" (263). Mrs. Hale and Mrs. Peters both understand what has

happened to Minnie, and this sympathetic understanding leads them to hide the box (291-292) from the men.

9. Students might need to know that the layers of quilts (top, bottom, and the stuffing layer in between) can be sewn together or they may be secured together with looped strings pulled from the bottom to the top; the ends of the strings are then tied into knots. The men have made fun of Minnie's quilting choice, to them another trivial female decision, but they overlook the fact that Minnie is obviously very good at tying knots (as in, for example, the rope around John's neck). Readers may also see meaning in that the three women are now firmly tied together, perhaps united with all women.

10. Mrs. Hale and Mrs. Peters are her jury in a case of spousal abuse, even more ironic because at that time, women could not serve on juries. By hiding the bird and remaining quiet, they have found Minnie innocent of first-degree murder. Students may wish to debate the ethics of their "verdict"; does the time of this story – early in the twentieth century when women had few legal rights—affect the students' view of Mrs. Hale and Mrs. Peters' action? Other, more modern, cases of domestic abuse might also play a role in this discussion.

Vocabulary

1. queer (32)—odd, unusual
2. ungainly (68)—lacking in grace or refinement; clumsy
3. conceded (202)—agreed, to give value to another's opinion or position
4. petticoat (267)—an undergarment used by women as a slip or to fill out a skirt, usually with ruffles
5. incisively (271)—with exactness or precision